m 3 2 11-11

"WITH SUN-TROD FACES AND HORN-GLOVED HANDS." [P. 113.

# FARM FESTIVALS

By WILL CARLETON

AUTHOR OF "FARM BALLADS" "FARM LEGENDS" ETC.

*ILLUSTRATED*

NEW YORK
HARPER & BROTHERS, PUBLISHERS
FRANKLIN SQUARE

TO

# SISTERS AND BROTHER

ALL GONE ON

THROUGH SAD, MYSTERIOUS MISTS

INTO

THE GREAT BRIGHTNESS

# PREFACE.

—◇◇◇—

NOT all the festivals of the farm have been attempted in these pages; there are still more in the author's heart than in his book.

Such only have been selected as might best help to express the thoughts, fancies, and memories which were uppermost in his mind, and (in a few cases) to garner certain poems already written.

Some of the characters were drawn from people the author has known—some of the incidents from scenes in which he has participated; but the names used are, of course, all fictitious, though taken at random from such as are likely to be found in any farming community.

With these few words of introduction, he respectfully presents to the public this third number of THE FARM SERIES, and will be more than pleased, should it gain as kind and generous a greeting as have its predecessors.

W. C.

# CONTENTS.

1

# ILLUSTRATIONS.

# FARM FESTIVALS.

---

## THE FESTIVAL OF REMINISCENCE;

OR,

## THE PIONEER MEETING.

### I.

WITHIN a grove, where maples strove
 To keep their sweet-tongued goods,
Met, worn with years, some pioneers—
 The Old Guard of the woods;
Who came once more to linger o'er
 The grim work of their primes,
Renewing here the grief and cheer
 Of happy, hard old times.
Rough clad were they—unkempt and gray—
 With lack of studied ease—
Yet beauty-strown with charms their own,
 Like brave old forest trees.
Their eyes seemed still to flash the will
 Of spirits sent to win;
Their hands were marred; their cheeks were scarred
 By deep wounds from within.

With awkward grace and earnest face
 Of effort-bought repose,
With troubled ease and shaking knees,
 Their president arose.

The crowd in view from him first drew
  That flustered word "Ahem!"
He who when found on equal ground,
  Could talk so free with them.
('Tis strange how one who well has known
  His friends, from day to day,
Those same ones fears, when he appears
  On higher ground than they!)
But he arose, and his snub nose
  Twanged with a sound immense;
Which bugle-blast about him cast,
  Gave him self-confidence.
And while a look of reverence took
  His anxious-wrinkled face,
He begged the good old elder would
  Invoke the throne of grace.

A sweet old man, of clean-cut plan
  And undissembling air,
Rose in his place, with fervent face,
  And made a business prayer.
He never threw his voice into
  A sad uncalled-for wail;
He ne'er aspired to make Heaven tired,
  With gossip weak and stale;
He did not ask a toilless task,
  Or claim undue reward,
He did not shout opinions out,
  Or "dance before The Lord";
He did not prate of town or state,
  Suggesting them by name;
With his calm voice, no precepts choice,
  Or general orders, came.—
Thanks—many a one—for favors done,
  Hopes—modest-clothed—for more,
Praise, love, and fear, and all sincere,
  And then his words were o'er.
So old was he, it seemed to me,
  In this strong, feeble prayer,

"THE OLD GUARD OF THE WOODS."

He knocked once more at Heaven's front door,
    And left his message there.

With side-turned head, the chairman said,
    "To help this meetin' 'long,
My eldest son, George Washington,
    Will perpetrate a song."
Uncouth of view, George W.
    Rose in his ample tracks,
And gave, in voice not over choice,
    The loud

## SONG OF THE AXE.

They called me off of the hard couch of my rest—
    "Wake up! wake up! for the morning breaks!" they said.
To the bath of the white-hot fire they bared my breast—
    The lash of the iron sledge fell on my head.
        Far and near
            My pain-cries bounded;
        Shrill and clear
            The anvils sounded;
        "Work!" they cried:
            "The day has broke!
        The forests wide
            Await the stroke
Of the serpent-spring of the woodman's cordy arm,
    As it flings the white-toothed axe against the tree;
The noon shall gleam on many a prosperous farm,
    And the growing grain the forest's child shall be."

I went to the streetless city of the wood—
    I carried there destruction's surest pang;
The tree that many a hundred years had stood,
    Now fell at the touch of my silver-gleaming fang.
        Far and wide
            My voice was calling;
        Every side
            The trees were falling;
    2

"Cease," I said,
  "Your barbarous cheer,
And bow the head,
  For death is near!"
And the oak-tree gazed at its steadily gaping wound,
  And nursed the stinging pain that it could not tell;
Then grandly drooped, with an agony-moaning sound,
  And dashed and crashed through the brush, and, thundering, fell.

Wherever are heard my voice's ominous sounds,
  The half-clad feet of the homeless millions run;
They pitch their tents of wood on my battle grounds—
  They eat the fruits of the work that I have done.
          Toil that dares
            Is tenfold glorious;
          All earth shares
            Its march victorious;
          "Haste!" it cries:
            "Your venturous deeds
          Will win a prize
            For human needs!"
So I strike the key-note of the national song
  Of empires that shall star through future years:
And the artist-tribes do but my strains prolong,
  And I am the pioneer of pioneers.

## II.

Came speeches, then, by withered men,
  In language brusque and plain;
And, as it happ'd, most of them tapped
  The reminiscence vein.
Age loves through ways of olden days
  With Memory's lamp to grope;
As proud Youth peers at future years,
  Lit by the torch of Hope.
How far between are Memory's scene
  And Hope's unclouded view!
False is each one, and overdone—
  Yet both are wondrous true.

And toward the close, there calmly rose
   A sad-eyed veteran hoary,
And with a fair and modest air,
   Told

### THE FIRST SETTLER'S STORY.

It ain't the funniest thing a man can do—
Existing in a country when it's new;
Nature—who moved in first—a good long while—
Has things already somewhat her own style,
And she don't want her woodland splendors battered,
Her rustic furniture broke up and scattered,
Her paintings, which long years ago were done
By that old splendid artist-king, the Sun,
Torn down and dragged in Civilization's gutter,
Or sold to purchase settlers' bread-and-butter.
She don't want things exposed, from porch to closet—
And so she kind o' nags the man who does it.
She carries in her pockets bags of seeds,
As general agent of the thriftiest weeds;
She sends her blackbirds, in the early morn,
To superintend his fields of planted corn;
She gives him rain past any duck's desire—
Then may be several weeks of quiet fire;
She sails mosquitoes—leeches perched on wings—
To poison him with blood-devouring stings;
She loves her ague-muscle to display,
And shake him up—say every other day;
With thoughtful, conscientious care, she makes
Those travellin' poison-bottles, rattlesnakes;
She finds time, 'mongst her other family cares,
To keep in stock good wild-cats, wolves, and bears;
She spurns his offered hand, with silent gibes,
And compromises with the Indian tribes
(For they who've wrestled with his bloody art
Say Nature always takes an Indian's part).
In short, her toil is every day increased,
To scare him out, and hustle him back East;

Till fin'lly, it appears to her some day,
That he has made arrangements for to stay;
Then she turns 'round, as sweet as anything,
And takes her new-made friend into the ring,
And changes from a snarl into a purr:
From mother-in-law to mother, as it were.

Well, when I first infested this retreat,
Things to my view looked frightful incomplete:
But Nature seemed quite cheerful, all about me,
A-carrying on her different trades without me.
These words the forest seemed at me to throw:
"Sit down and rest awhile before you go;"
From bees to trees the whole woods seemed to say,
"You're welcome here till you can get away,
But not for time of any large amount;
So don't be hanging round on our account."
But I had come with heart-thrift in my song,
And brought my wife and plunder right along;
I hadn't a round-trip ticket to go back,
And if I had, there wasn't no railroad track;
And drivin' east was what I couldn't endure:
I hadn't started on a circular tour.

My girl-wife was as brave as she was good,
And helped me every blessèd way she could;
She seemed to take to every rough old tree,
As sing'lar as when first she took to me.
She kep' our little log-house neat as wax;
And once I caught her fooling with my axe.
She learned a hundred masculine things to do:
She aimed a shot-gun pretty middlin' true,
Although, in spite of my express desire,
She always shut her eyes before she'd fire.
She hadn't the muscle (though she *had* the heart)
In out-door work to take an active part;
Though in our firm of Duty & Endeavor,
She wasn't no silent partner whatsoever.

"HER LITTLE SCRUB CLASS IN THE SUNDAY-SCHOOL."

When I was logging, burning, choppin' wood—
She'd linger 'round, and help me all she could,
And kept me fresh-ambitious all the while,
And lifted tons, just with her voice and smile.
With no desire my glory for to rob,
She used to stan' around and boss the job;
And when first-class success my hands befell,
Would proudly say, "*We* did that pretty well!"
She *was* delicious, both to hear and see—
That pretty wife-girl that kep' house for me!

Sundays, we didn't propose, for lack o' church,
To have our souls left wholly in the lurch;
And so I shaved and dressed up, well's I could,
And did a day's work trying to be good.
My wife was always bandbox-sleek; and when
Our fat old bull's-eye watch said half-past ten
('Twas always varying from the narrow way,
And lied on Sundays, same as any day),
The family Bible from its high perch started
(The one her mother gave her when they parted),
The hymn-book, full of music-balm and fire—
The one she used to sing in in the choir—
One I sang with her from—I've got it yet—
The very first time that we *really* met;
(I recollect, when first our voices gibed,
A feeling that declines to be described!
And when our eyes met—near the second verse—
A kind of old-acquaintance look in hers,
And something went from mine, which, I declare,
I never even knew before was there—
And when our hands touched—slight as slight could be—
A streak o' sweetened lightnin' thrilled through me!
But that's enough of that; perhaps, even now,
You'll think I'm softer than the law 'll allow;
But you'll protect an old man with his age,
For yesterday I turned my eightieth page;
Besides, there'd be less couples falling out
If such things were more freely talked about.)

Well, we would take these books, sit down alone,
And have a two-horse meeting, all our own;
And read our verses, sing our sacred rhymes,
And make it seem a good deal like old times.
But finally across her face there'd glide
A sort of sorry shadow from inside;
And once she dropped her head, like a tired flower,
Upon my arm, and cried a half an hour.
I humored her until she had it out,
And didn't ask her what it was about.

I knew right well: our reading, song, and prayer
Had brought the old times back, too true and square.
The large attended meetings morn and night;
The spiritual and mental warmth and light;
Her father, in his pew, next to the aisle;
Her mother, with the mother of her smile;
Her brothers' sly, forbidden Sunday glee;
Her sisters, e'en a'most as sweet as she;
Her girl and boy friends, not too warm or cool;
Her little scrub class in the Sunday-school;
The social, and the singings and the ball;
And happy home-cheer waiting for them all—
These marched in close procession through her mind,
And didn't forget to leave their tracks behind.
You married men—there's many in my view—
Don't think your wife can all wrap up in you,
Don't deem, though close her life to yours may grow,
That you are all the folks she wants to know;
Or think your stitches form the only part
Of the crochet-work of a woman's heart.
Though married souls each other's lives may burnish,
Each needs some help the other cannot furnish.

Well, neighborhoods meant counties, in those days;
The roads didn't have accommodating ways;
And maybe weeks would pass before she'd see—
And much less talk with—any one but me.
The Indians sometimes showed their sun-baked faces,
But they didn't teem with conversational graces;
Some ideas from the birds and trees she stole,
But 'twasn't like talking with a human soul;
And finally I thought that I could trace
A half heart-hunger peering from her face.
Then she would drive it back, and shut the door;
Of course that only made me see it more.
'Twas hard to see her give her life to mine,
Making a steady effort not to pine;
'Twas hard to hear that laugh bloom out each minute,
And recognize the seeds of sorrow in it.

No misery makes a close observer mourn,
Like hopeless grief with hopeful courage borne;
There's nothing sets the sympathies to paining,
Like a complaining woman, uncomplaining!
It always draws my breath out into sighs,
To see a brave look in a woman's eyes.

Well, she went on, as plucky as could be,
Fighting the foe she thought I did not see,
And using her heart-horticultural powers
To turn that forest to a bed of flowers.
You can not check an unadmitted sigh,
And so I had to soothe her on the sly,
And secretly to help her draw her load;
And soon it came to be an up-hill road.
Hard work bears hard upon the average pulse,
Even with satisfactory results;
But when effects are scarce, the heavy strain
Falls dead and solid on the heart and brain.
And when we're bothered, it will oft occur
We seek blame-timber; and I lit on her;
And looked at her with daily lessening favor,
For what I knew she couldn't help, to save her.
(We often—what our minds should blush with shame for –
Blame people most for what they're least to blame for.)
Then there'd a misty, jealous thought occur,
Because I wasn't Earth and Heaven to her,
And all the planets that about us hovered,
And several more that hadn't been discovered;
And my hard muscle-labor, day by day,
Deprived good-nature of the right of way;
And 'tain't no use—this trying to conceal
From hearts that love us—what our own hearts feel;
They can't escape close observation's mesh—
And thoughts have tongues that are not made of flesh.
And so ere long she caught the half-grown fact:
Commenced observing how I didn't act;
And silently began to grieve and doubt
O'er old attentions now sometimes left out—

Some kind caress—some little petting ways—
Commenced a-staying in on rainy days
(I did not see 't so clear then, I'll allow;
But I can trace it rather acc'rate now);
And Discord, when he once had called and seen us,
Came round quite often, and edged in between us.

One night, I came from work unusual late,
Too hungry and too tired to feel first-rate—
Her supper struck me wrong (though I'll allow
She hadn't much to strike with, anyhow);
And when I went to milk the cows, and found
They'd wandered from their usual feeding ground,
And maybe 'd left a few long miles behind 'em,
Which I must copy, if I meant to find 'em,
Flash-quick the stay-chains of my temper broke,
And in a trice these hot words I had spoke:
"You ought to 've kept the animals in view,
And drove 'em in; you'd nothing else to do.
The heft of all our life on me must fall;
You just lie round, and let me do it all."

That speech—it hadn't been gone a half a minute,
Before I saw the cold black poison in it;
And I'd have given all I had, and more,
To 've only safely got it back in-door.
I'm now what most folks "well-to-do" would call:
I feel to-day as if I'd give it all,
Provided I through fifty years might reach,
And kill and bury that half-minute speech.
Boys flying kites haul in their white-winged birds;
You can't do that way when you're flying words.
Things that we think may sometimes fall back dead;
But God himself can't kill them when they're said.

She handed back no words, as I could hear;
She didn't frown—she didn't shed a tear;
Half proud, half crushed, she stood and looked me o'er,
Like some one she had never seen before!

But such a sudden anguish-lit surprise
I never viewed before in human eyes.
(I've seen it oft enough since, in a dream ;
It sometimes wakes me, like a midnight scream !)

That night, while theoretically sleeping,
I half heard and half felt that she was weeping ;
And my heart then projected a design
To softly draw her face up close to mine,
And beg of her forgiveness to bestow,
For saying what we both knew wasn't so.
I've got enough of this world's goods to do me,
And make my nephews painfully civil to me :
I'd give it all to know she only knew
How near I came to what was square and true.
But somehow, every single time I'd try,
Pride would appear, and kind o' catch my eye,
And hold me, on the edge of my advance,
With the cold steel of one sly, scornful glance.

Next morning, when, stone-faced, but heavy-hearted,
With dinner pail and sharpened axe I started
Away for my day's work—she watched the door,
And followed me half-way to it or more ;
And I was just a-turning round at this,
And asking for my usual good-bye kiss ;
But on her lip I saw a proudish curve,
And in her eye a shadow of reserve ;
And she had shown—perhaps half unawares—
Some little independent breakfast airs—
And so the usual parting didn't occur,
Although her eyes invited me to her,
Or rather half invited me ; for she
Didn't advertise to furnish kisses free :
You always had—that is, I had—to pay
Full market price, and go more 'n half the way.
So, with a short "Good-bye," I shut the door,
And left her as I never had before.

Now, when a man works with his muscle smartly,
It makes him up into machinery, partly;
And any trouble he may have on hand
Gets deadened like, and easier to stand.
And though the memory of last night's mistake
Bothered me with a dull and heavy ache,
I all the forenoon gave my strength full rein,
And made the wounded trees bear half the pain.
But when at noon my lunch I came to eat,
Put up by her so delicately neat—
Choicer, somewhat, than yesterday's had been,
And some fresh, sweet-eyed pansies she'd put in—
"Tender and pleasant thoughts," I knew they meant—
It seemed as if her kiss with me she'd sent;
Then I became once more her humble lover,
And said, "To-night I'll ask forgiveness of her."

I went home over-early on that eve,
Having contrived to make myself believe,
By various signs I kind o' knew and guessed,
A thunder-storm was coming from the west.
('Tis strange, when one sly reason fills the heart,
How many honest ones will take its part;
A dozen first-class reasons said 'twas right
That I should strike home early on that night.)

Half out of breath, the cabin door I swung,
With tender heart-words trembling on my tongue;
But all within looked desolate and bare;
My house had lost its soul—she was not there!
A pencilled note was on the table spread,
And these are something like the words it said:
"The cows have strayed away again, I fear;
I watched them pretty close; don't scold me, dear.
And where they are, I think I *nearly* know:
I heard the bell not very long ago—
*       *       *       *       *       *       *
I've hunted for them all the afternoon;
I'll try once more—I think I'll find them soon.

Dear, if a burden I have been to you,
And haven't helped you as I ought to do,
Let old-time memories my forgiveness plead;
I've tried to do my best—I have, indeed.
Darling, piece out with love the strength I lack,
And have kind words for me when I get back."

Scarce did I give this letter sight and tongue—
Some swift-blown rain-drops to the window clung,
And from the clouds a rough, deep growl proceeded;
My thunder-storm had come, now 'twasn't needed.
I rushed out-door; the air was stained with black;
Night had come early, on the storm-cloud's back.
And every thing kept dimming to the sight,
Save when the clouds threw their electric light;
When, for a flash, so clean-cut was the view,
I'd think I saw her—knowing 'twas not true.
Through my small clearing dashed wide sheets of spray,
As if the ocean waves had lost their way;
Scarcely a pause the thunder-battle made,
In the bold clamor of its cannonade.
And she, while I was sheltered, dry and warm,
Was somewhere in the clutches of this storm!
She who, when storm-frights found her at her best,
Had always hid her white face on my breast!

My dog, who'd skirmished 'round me all the day,
Now, crouched and whimpering, in a corner lay;
I dragged him by the collar to the wall—
I pressed his quivering muzzle to a shawl—
"Track her, old boy!" I shouted: and he whined,
Matched eyes with me, as if to read my mind—
Then with a yell went tearing through the wood.
I followed him, as faithful as I could.
No pleasure-trip was that, through flood and flame!
We raced with death;—we hunted noble game.
All night we dragged the woods without avail;
The ground got drenched—we could not keep the trail.

Three times again my cabin home I found,
Half hoping she might be there, safe and sound;
But each time 'twas an unavailing care:
My house had lost its soul; she was not there!

When, climbing the wet trees, next morning-sun
Laughed at the ruin that the night had done,
Bleeding and drenched—by toil and sorrow bent—
Back to what used to be my home I went.
But, as I neared our little clearing-ground—
Listen!—I heard the cow-bell's tinkling sound;
The cabin door was just a bit ajar;
It gleamed upon my glad eyes like a star!
"Brave heart," I said, "for such a fragile form!
She made them guide her homeward through the storm!"
Such pangs of joy I never felt before:
"You've come!" I shouted, and rushed through the door.

Yes, she had come—and gone again.—She lay
With all her young life crushed and wrenched away—
Lay—the heart-ruins of our home among—
Not far from where I killed her with my tongue.
The rain drops glittered 'mid her hair's long strands,
The forest-thorns had torn her feet and hands,
And 'midst the tears—brave tears—that one could trace
Upon the pale but sweetly resolute face,
I once again the mournful words could read—
"I've tried to do my best—I have, indeed."

And now I'm mostly done; my story's o'er;
Part of it never breathed the air before.
'Tisn't over-usual, it must be allowed,
To volunteer heart-history to a crowd,
And scatter 'mongst them confidential tears,
But you'll protect an old man with his years;
And wheresoe'er this story's voice can reach,
This is the sermon I would have it preach:

Boys flying kites haul in their white-winged birds;
You can't do that way when you're flying words.

"Careful with fire," is good advice, we know:
"Careful with words," is ten times doubly so.
Thoughts unexpressed may sometimes fall back dead;
But God himself can't kill them when they're said!

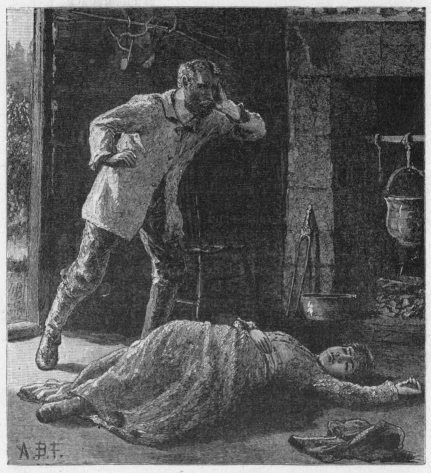

"YES, SHE HAD COME—AND GONE AGAIN."

You have my life-grief: do not think a minute
'Twas told to take up time. There's business in it.
It sheds advice; whoe'er will take and live it,
Is welcome to the pain it costs to give it.

## III.

With added calm, untangling from
    The twists of bench repose,
When silence called, serene and bald,
    The President arose;
And with bowed head he humbly said,
    "To help this meetin' 'long,
My second one, James Madison,
    Will now submit a song."
James M. appeared, his infant beard
    Hopes for the future shedding,
And sung in strains of anxious pains

### ELIPHALET CHAPIN'S WEDDING.

'Twas when the leaves of Autumn were by tempest-fingers picked,
Eliphalet Chapin started to become a benedict;
With an ancient two-ox wagon to bring back his new-found goods,
He hawed and gee'd and floundered through some twenty miles o'
        woods;
With prematrimonial ardor he his hornéd steeds did press,
But Eliphalet's wedding journey didn't bristle with success.
            Oh no, woe, woe!
            With candor to digress,
Eliphalet's wedding journey didn't tremble with success.

He had not carried five miles his mouth-disputed face,
When his wedding garments parted in some inconvenient place;
He'd have given both his oxen to a wife that now was dead,
For her company two minutes with a needle and a thread.
But he pinned them up, with twinges of occasional distress,
Feeling that his wedding wouldn't be a carnival of dress:
            "Haw, Buck!"
            Gee, Bright!
            Derned pretty mess!"
No; Eliphalet was not strictly a spectacular success.

He had not gone a ten-mile when a wheel demurely broke,
A disunited family of felloe, hub, and spoke;

It joined, with flattering prospects, the Society of Wrecks;
And he had to cut a sapling, and insert it 'neath the "ex."

"NOW, WHEN HE DROVE HIS EQUIPAGE UP TO HIS SWEETHEART'S DOOR."

So he plowed the hills and valleys with that Doric wheel and tire,
Feeling that his wedding journey was not all he could desire.
        "Gee, Bright!
        G'long, Buck!"
        He shouted, hoarse with ire:
No; Eliphalet's wedding journey none in candor could admire!

He had not gone fifteen miles with extended face forlorn,
When Night lay down upon him hard, and kept him there till morn;
And when the daylight chuckled at the gloom within his mind,
One ox was "Strayed or Stolen," and the other hard to find.
So yoking Buck as usual, he assumed the part of Bright
(Constituting a menagerie diverting to the sight);
   With " Haw, Buck !
   Gee, Buck !
   Sha'n't get there till night !"
No ; Eliphalet's wedding journey was not one intense delight.

Now, when he drove his equipage up to his sweetheart's door,
The wedding guests had tired and gone, just half an hour before;
The preacher had from sickness an unprofitable call,
And had sent a voice proclaiming that he couldn't come at all;
The parents had been prejudiced by some one, more or less,
And the sire the bridegroom greeted with a different word from
  " bless."
   " Blank your head,
   You blank !" he said ;
   " We'll break this off, I guess !"
No ; Eliphalet's wedding was not an unqualified success.

Now, when the bride saw him arrive, she shook her crimson locks,
And vowed to goodness gracious she would never wed an ox ;
And with a vim deserving rather better social luck,
She eloped that day by daylight with a swarthy Indian "buck,"
With the presents in the pockets of her woolen wedding-dress;
And " Things ain't mostly with me," quoth Eliphalet, " I confess."
   No—no ;
   As things go,
   No fair mind 'twould impress,
That Eliphalet Chapin's wedding was an unalloyed success.

Eliphalet Chapin started home—

### IV.

  Once more unbent the President,
  With face grown sadly long, .
   3

And said, "How many more, if any,
  Such verses has that song?"
With smile unchanged, the minstrel ranged
  Four fingers and a thumb,
And said, "There'll be just ninety-three
  More stanzas yet to come."
With look of dread, the father said,
  "You need not sing 'em here,
But get your man home, if you can,
  Some time this coming year."
Without a frown, James M. sat down,
  Stripped of his vocal glory;
And then an old rough patriarch told


### THE SECOND SETTLER'S STORY.

A han'some night, with the trees snow-white,
  And the time say ten or more,
Saw wife and me, with a well-fed glee,
  Drive home from Jackson's store.
There was wife and I, and some things folks buy,
  And our horses and our sleigh;
And the moon went along with its lantern strong,
  And lit us as light as day.
We'd made roads good, drawin' logs and wood,
  For thirty years ago;
And the wear and tear had sustained repair
  From Road Commissioner Snow.
As we trotted along, our two-thread song
  Wove in with the sleigh-bells' chimes;
Our laugh run free, and it seemed to me
  We was havin' first-rate times.

I said "first-rate," but I do not say 't
  On a thoroughly thorough plan;
I had won my wife, in legitimate strife,
  Away from her first young man.
'Twas a perfect rout, and a fair cut-out,
  With nothing sneaky or wrong;

But I wondered so as to whether or no
  She had brought her *heart* along!
A woman half-won is worse than none,
  With another man keepin' part;
It's nothin' to gain her body and brain,
  If she can't throw in her heart.
And I felt and thought that I sometimes caught
  A chillness out o' her mind;
She was too much prone to thinkin' alone,
  And rather too coldly kind.

But things seemed right this partic'lar night,
  More so than with average folks;
And we filled the air with music to spare,
  And complimentary jokes.
Till, as I reckoned, about a second
  All happened to be still—
A cry like the yell of hounds from hell
  Came over a neighboring hill.
It cut like a blade through the leafless shade;
  It chilled us stiff with dread;
We looked loud cries in each other's eyes—
  And—"*Wolves!*" was all we said.
The wolf! grim scamp and forest-tramp—
  Why made, I never could see;
Beneath brute level—half dog, half devil—
  The Indian-animal, he!
And this was a year with a winter more drear
  Than any we'd ever known;
It was '43; and the wolves, you see,
  Had a famine of their own.
That season, at least, of man and beast
  They captured many a one;
And we knew, by the bite of their voice that night,
  That they hadn't come out for fun.

My horses felt need of all their speed,
  And every muscle strained:

But, with all they could do, I felt and knew
    That the hungry devils gained.
'Twas but two miles more to our own house door,
    Where shelter we would find,
When I saw the pack close on to our track,
    Not a hundred yards behind.
Then I silent prayed: "O God! for aid—
    Just a trifle—I request!
Just give us, You know, an even show,
    And I'll undertake the rest."
Then I says to my wife, "Now drive for life!
    They're a-comin' over-nigh!
And I will stand, gun and axe in hand,
    And be the first to die."
As the ribbons she took, she gave me a look
    Sweet memory makes long-lived:
I thought, "I'll allow she loves me now;
    The rest of her heart has arrived."
I felt I could fight the whole o' the night,
    And never flinch or tire!
In danger, mind you, a woman behind you
    Can turn your blood to fire.

When they reached the right spot, I left 'em a shot,
    But it wasn't a steady aim—
'Twasn't really mine—and they tipped me a whine,
    And came on all the same.
Their leader sped a little ahead,
    Like a gray knife from its sheath;
With a resolute eye, and a hungry cry,
    And an excellent set of teeth.
A moment I gazed—my axe I raised—
    It hissed above my head—
Crunching low and dull, it split his skull,
    And the villain fell back dead!
It checked them there, and a minute to spare
    We had, and a second besides:
With rites unsaid they buried their dead
    In the graves of their own lank hides.

"COME ON!" I SAID, "WITH YOUR FIERCE LIPS RED."

They made for him a funeral grim—
    Himself the unbaked meat;
And when they were through with their barbecue,
    They started for more to eat!

With voices aflame, once more they came;
    But faster still we sped,
And we and our traps dashed home perhaps
    A half a minute ahead.
My wife I bore through the open door,
    Then turned to the hearth clean swept,
Where a log-fire glowed in its brick abode—
    By my mother faithfully kept;
From its depths raising two fagots blazing,
    I leaped like lightning back;
I dashed the brands, with my blistering hands,
    In the teeth of the howling pack.
"Come on!" I said, "with your fierce lips red,
    Flecked white with poison foam!
Waltz to me now, and just notice how
    A man fights for his home!"
They shrunk with fright from the feel and sight
    O' this sudden volley of flame;
With a yell of dread, they sneaked and fled,
    As fast as ever they came.

As I turned around, my wife I found
    Not the eighth of an inch away:
She looked so true and tender, I knew
    That her heart had come—to stay.
She nestled more nigh, with love-lit eye,
    And passionate-quivering lip;
And I saw that the lout that I cut out
    Had probably lost his grip.
Doubt moved away, for a permanent stay,
    And never was heard of more!
My soul must own that it had not known
    The soul of my wife before.

As I staunched the steam on my foaming team,
　　These thoughts hitched to my mind:
Below or above some woman's love,
　　How little in life we find!
A man 'll go far to plant a star
　　Where fame's wide sky is thrown,
But a longer way, for some woman to say,
　　"I love you for my own."
And oft as I've worked, this thought has lurked
　　'Round me, with substantial aid:
Of the best and worst men have done since first
　　This twofold world was made:
Of the farms they've cleared—of the buildin's reared—
　　The city splendors wrought—
Of the battle-field, where, loth to yield,
　　The right 'gainst the right has fought;
Of the measured strains of the lightning-trains,
　　The clack of the quick-spoke wire—
Of the factory's clash and the forge's flash,
　　An' the furnace's plumes of fire;
Be 't great or small—nine-tenths of all
　　Of every trade and art,
Be 't right or wrong—is merely a song
　　To win some woman's heart.


## V.

With haste well meant, the President
　　Laboriously arose,
And said, "'Tis near the time, I fear,
　.　This meetin' ought to close.
But ere we grieve this spot to leave,
　　To help the meetin' 'long,
My youngest one, T. Jefferson,
　　Will *contribute* a song."
Like sheep that fly, when lingers nigh
　　Some foe their leader fears;
Like boys at play, when far away
　　Parental wrath appears;

Like any thing that fright can bring
    Into the average throng,
The crowd withdrew from casual view,
    To dodge the threatened song.
With better pluck than vocal luck,
    And face of hardy cheer,
Young Thomas J. closed out the day
    With

## SLEEP, OLD PIONEER!

When the Spring-time touch is lightest,
When the Summer-eyes are brightest,
    Or the Autumn sings most drear;
When the Winter's hair is whitest,
    Sleep, old pioneer!
Safe beneath the sheltering soil,
    Late enough you crept;
You were weary of the toil
    Long before you slept.
Well you paid for every blessing,
    Bought with grief each day of cheer:
Nature's arms around you pressing,
Nature's lips your brow caressing,
    Sleep, old pioneer!

When the hill of toil was steepest,
When the forest-frown was deepest,
    Poor, but young, you hastened here;
Came where solid hope was cheapest—
    Came—a pioneer.
Made the western jungles view
    Civilization's charms;
Snatched a home for yours and you,
    From the lean tree-arms.
Toil had never cause to doubt you—
    Progress' path you helped to clear:
But To-day forgets about you,
And the world rides on without you—
    Sleep, old pioneer!

Careless crowds go daily past you,
Where *their* future fate has cast you,
   Leaving not a sigh or tear;
And your wonder-works outlast you—
   Brave old pioneer!
Little care the selfish throng
   Where your heart is hid,
Though they thrive upon the strong,
   Resolute work it did.
But *our* memory-eyes have found you,
   And we hold you grandly dear;
With no work-day woes to wound you—
With the peace of GOD around you—
   Sleep, old pioneer!

"SLEEP, OLD PIONEER!"

# THE FESTIVAL OF PRAISE;

## OR

## THANKSGIVING-DAY.

'Tis in the thriftful Autumn days,
   When earth is overdone,
And forest trees have caught the blaze
   Thrown at them by the sun,
When up the gray smoke puffs and curls
   From cottage chimney-lips,
And oft the driving storm unfurls
   The black sails of his ships,
Or Indian Summer, dimly fair,
   May walk the valleys through,
And paint the glass walls of the air
   In tints of dreamy blue,
When Summer is mislaid and lost
   Among the leaflets dead,
And Winter, in white words of frost,
   Has telegraphed ahead,
When far afield the farmer blows
   His fingers, numbed with cold,
And robs from stately corn-hill rows,
   Their pocket-books of gold,
When, with a weird and horn-like note,
   The cloud-geese southward fly,
In branches leafed with wings, that float
   Along the liquid sky,
When to their meals the gobblers strut,
   In gastronomic mood,

And little dream that they are but
 A food-devouring food,
When chains adorn the chimney-vests,
 Of apples hung to dry,
And in his barrel-coffin rests
 The porker, doomed to die,
Or, still the recent cruel sport
 Of knife-engendered pangs,
His blushing corpse, with lessened port,
 Upon the gallows hangs;
'Tis then good prosperous folks display
 A reverential cheer,
And thank their Maker one whole day
 For all the previous year.

The President proclaims that thus
 His duty does direct;
The Governor has written us
 Unto the same effect;
Now let the housewife's nets be cast,
 And all the poultry kind
Begin to realize, at last,
 For what they were designed;
Now rob your fowl-yards of their game,
 Till tables groan, anon,
That they who eat may do the same
 A little farther on;
Now let your clans of cousins meet,
 And talk their blessings o'er,
And thank The Lord for what they eat,
 By eating all the more;
Now let your industry's reward
 Achieve a fair display,
And hearts and stomachs thank The Lord,
 Alternately all day!

The patriarch-farmer, worn and tanned,
 Has all his heart alive

'TIS IN THE THRIFTFUL AUTUMN DAYS.

To sight his married children, and
　　Assist them to arrive.
The open gate he rushes through,
　　With step surprising fast,
And hails the first that drives in view,
　　"Ho! ho! you've come at last!"
He helps his daughter-in-law alight,
　　With elephantine grace,
And kisses hard each toddling wight,
　　All o'er its tender face;
And soon as "Mother" comes and throws
　　The woman-greeting-scream,
Together with his son he goes,
　　To help him stall his team.
So constantly new-comers gain
　　Old greeting from the sire,
And soon they form a sparkling chain,
　　Around a blazing fire.
And Reminiscence deftly trips
　　Them and "old times" between,
And tempts their conversation-lips
　　With memories sweet and keen.
Old happenings are handled o'er,
　　In stories somewhat true;
The family all is raised once more,
　　Here in an hour or two.
There is no speech too dull to quote—
　　The last tale is the best;
Biography and anecdote
　　Are each an honored guest.
The family-liar may be here;
　　And is not greatly grieved,
To know his tales, unduly queer,
　　Are kindly disbelieved;
A-many words are gayly spoke,
　　Illiterately bright;
And every crippled, veteran joke,
　　Is stirred up to the sight;

4

And tales are told of childhoods tipped
    With follies wisely hid,
And how the good boy oft was whipped
    For what the bad one did;
Of many a brain and muscle bout,
    By plastic memory fed,
In which the one who tells comes out
    Invariably ahead
(For people's lives, you know full well,
    Two sets of things recall:
The one of which they often tell,
    The other not at all);
The children romping rush and lurk,
    And demonstrate their lungs;
The women ply their knitting-work
    With unimpeded tongues.
Live fast, you selfish, thankful throng,
    For life to-day is fair,
And when the dinner comes along,
    Take in a goodly share!
The future keeps just out of view,
    And sorrow waits ahead;
There may be days when some of you
    Will beg a bit of bread.
The blessings of this day do not
    Secure a future one;
This is to thank The Lord for what
    He has already done.
And every laugh, however gay,
    By grief shall yet be quelled;
O'er each heart that is here to-day
    A funeral must be held.
Laugh on again, with careless voice,
    As soon as grace is said!
God loves to see His folks rejoice,
    No matter what's ahead.
You're sure of this Thanksgiving-day,
    Whose blessings on you fall;

"THE WOMEN PLY THEIR KNITTING-WORK."

A million thanks you should display
    For having lived at all.
Grief should be checked, with crafty plan,
    But ne'er by dreading nursed;
Care for the future all you can,
    Then let it do its worst!

The remnants of the poultry tribes
    Lugubriously confer;
Each selfish-sad the loss describes
    That worries him or her.
They who survive man's greedy choice—
    The thinnest of the clans—
With half raised foot and trembling voice,
    Discuss their future plans.
The turkey-orphan now and then
    Around her wildly looks;
Her sire is in yon tyrant's den:
    She smells him as he cooks.
The mother of the crowing wights
    Whose necks were lately wrung,
Leaves her spasmodic appetites,
    And plies her mournful tongue;
Or scratches absently about,
    Her luckless prey to view,
Forgetting, as she picks them out,
    That worms have mothers, too.
Her helpmeet, whose defiant crow
    Struck morning's earliest chimes,
Has left her side not long ago,
    And gone to warmer climes;
Her dearest friend of heart and kith,
    Her gossip and her aid,
The one that she changed cackles with
    Whenever either laid,
Has very suddenly moved on—
    With close-tied yellow legs—
To where, in days forever gone,
    She shipped so many eggs.

The hateful Now each moment mocks
    The over-happy Then;
Through sorrow's vale she sadly stalks,
    A crushed and broken hen.
Cheer up, old girl, and do not mind
    Fate's death-envenomed gibes!
God's bird-regards are not confined
    Unto the sparrow tribes.
By Him your shrill, queer mercy-prayer
    Was never once unheard;
He built you with as curious care
    As any other bird.
Fling off the grief that round you crept,
    Your cherished loves to lose;
Contact with friends is naught except
    A list of interviews;
And each and all must have an end—
    Stars rise, when others set—
If you live right, old speckled friend,
    You have a future yet.
Brush by the care that blocks your way;
    Strike a progressive mood!
Fly round, and make a nest, and lay,
    And hatch another brood!

The pauper will, as like as not,
    This festive day abhor,
And try to find what he has got
    To thank his Maker for.
With grim suspense of gratitude
    He views his last disease,
His ragged bed and broken food,
    And says, "It isn't these!"
He brushes, with his mournful eye,
    An ancient coat or hat,
And, standing back, with rueful sigh,
    Reflects, "It isn't that!"
He thinks of various friends he had,
    Who do not stand him true;

And, with a frown indignant sad,
    Remarks, " It isn't you !"
And still, he knows his meal to-day
    May show unusual cheer,
For Charity, when people pray,
    Creeps softly up to hear ;
And when their eye she slyly brings
    To their abundant shelves,
They send the paupers various things
    They do not want themselves.
But food bestowed is apt to be
    Unshapely to the eye,
And something of a parody
    On food that people buy.
Though may be given with good grace,
    And motive quite sincere,
The poor of the provision race
    Comes often also here :
The fowl, unclogged with fleshly pelf ;
    The bread-loaf underdone ;
The hash, a dinner of itself—
    Ten courses merged in one ;
The steak, once stoutly clinging nigh
    Some over-agéd bull ;
The meek and lowly veteran pie,
    Of reminiscence full.
But emptiness must ever yet
    Deem any filling rare ;
And stomachs love to work which get
    Much leisure time to spare.
With hearts that thanks can well afford,
    They gather, hungry clan,
Around the mildly-festal board,
    And do the best they can.
Here two old men, of meek intent,
    The past are dwelling on :
How they might have done different,
    If they had different done ;

They look back, and discern the cause
    Of each misfortune past,
And whose rascality it was
    That ruined them at last;
Ah, me! they might be wealthy men,
    With honors on their brow,
If they had calculated then
    As well as they do now!
The idiot in a corner lurks,
    And eats in bland disgrace;
Perhaps because his good mind works
    In an unhandy place.
You idiot boy, I like you much!
    Relationship I find;
Perhaps, indeed, we all are such
    To the celestial mind.
Perchance the charter angels call
    Us fit for laughter's ban,
Because we've fallen, since The Fall,
    A good deal lower than
Themselves, whose sails have had a chance
    At Heaven's progressive breeze,
While we 'gainst headwinds must advance,
    And toss on passion-seas.
You idiot boy, be vaguely glad;
    Your puzzled griefs discharge!
You have some rich relations, lad;
    Your family is large.
I rather think, that through some trade
    Not understood below,
Arrangements some time will be made
    To give your mind a show.
The oldwife feebly gnaws a bone—
    Her wits are half awhirl;
To-day she is a withered crone:
    She was a handsome girl.
Here is a drudge who's never shirked
    Her duty, it appears;

And for herself has only worked
    In these her feebler years.
Here is—but let us turn away
    From life's pain-printed leaf!
I have known comely hair turn gray
    With other people's grief.
Good-bye, dear ones! for you are dear
    To souls that yearn above;
If graves could open, you would hear
    Some genuine words of love.
The smiles that once your brows caressed
    Are still upon you thrown;
Your lips are yet by love-lips pressed;
    'Tis but the types are gone.
Good-bye, dear ones! for you are dear
    To One most high of place;
And He, with research long and clear,
    Has studied up your case!
He knows your mind and body pains,
    And when to soothe them out;
He knows what yet for you remains;
    He knows what He's about.
Your humble path is not agleam
    At this praise-spangled date;
Your thank-material none can deem
    Bewilderingly great;
But some day, when the time is fit—
    On some joy-lighted morn—
You'll thank Him for the whole of it,
    As sure as you are born!

The God above! what can we say
    Or do, with eyes so dim,
To make this Thursday-Sabbath day
    Thanksgiving-day to him?
What love, though grace and beauty clad,
    Can thrills to Him impart,
Who all the love has always had
    Of every brain-fed heart?

What can we sing to One whose verse
    Eternal song unbars?
What give to Him whose cloud-fringed purse
    Is crammed with gleaming stars?
A doubly pious way consists,
    When we our thanks would bring,
In recollecting He exists
    In every living thing;
That when or beast or man we touch
    With pity-helping care,
'Tis known in heaven just as much
    As if we did it there;
That when our voice in kind behalf
    Of any grief is heard,
Heaven's wondrous gold-foiled phonograph
    Is taking every word;
That when a heart the earth-heart serves,
    Of diamond or clod,
It thrills the universe's nerves,
    And glads the soul of God.

# THE FESTIVAL OF GOOD CHEER;

OR,

## CHRISTMAS MONOLOGUES.

### [FARMER.]

Blow—blow—bushels o' snow—
   As if you had lost your senses!
Rake with your might long winrows white,
   Along o' my walls·an' fences!
Hover and crowd, ye black-faced cloud!
   Your look 's with comfort mingled;
The more o' ye falls on these strong walls,
   The better my house is shingled.
Swarm, swarm, pale bees o' the storm!
   You bid the world look whiter;
Your very ire but pokes my fire,
   And makes the blaze burn brighter!

I ha' worked away more 'n one hot day,
   With the harvest-forge a-glowing,
To kindle the cheer of Summer here,
   When cold winds should be blowing.
I ha' braced my form 'gainst many a storm,
   When the gale blew helter-skelter—
O'er side-hills steep, through snow-drifts deep,
   I ha' climbed, to make this shelter.
My debts are raised, The Lord be praised!
   They left my old heart lighter;
That mortgage I fed to the fire-mouths red—
   And it made the flame burn brighter!

There's a smile that speaks, in the plump red cheeks
    Of the apples in these dishes;
They go down square, with a business air
    Of consultin' my stomach's wishes.
I am feelin' the charms of comfort's arms,
    Which never opened wider,

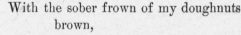

        With the sober frown of my doughnuts
            brown,
        And the laugh of my sweet-kept
            cider.
    (Of course I know that this all must go,
        In a whirl of death or sorrow;
    But there's nothing lost in the work it
            cost,
        If I knew I should die to-morrow!)

    My mind will play, this Christmas-day,
        Round the sad-faced little stranger
    That smiled on them at Bethlehem;
        And I wish it had been my manger!
    I'd ha' told 'em square to get out o' there,
        For I hadn't o'er-much o' shed-room,
    And move that lad and what else they
            had,
        Straight into my parlor bedroom.
    'Twas a story too true, and stranger, too,
        Than fairy tale or fable;
    An awkward thing for that preacher-
            king
        To be tossed about in a stable!

'Twould ha' been a joy to ha' given that boy
    A quiet heart ovation,
Before He was known as heir to a throne,
    Or had struck His reputation.
But I think I've read some words He said,
    In one of His printed sermons,
"Of the least of these," in which one sees
    The poor, the weak, the infirm 'uns;

So I b'lieve I know ten turkeys or
    so—
  Each one a fat old sinner—
Who'll wend their way to the poor-
    house t'day,
  And probably stay to dinner.

Growl—growl—ye storm-dogs, howl
  As if ye was tryin' to tree me!
For all o' your tricks, my grown-up
    chicks
  Are comin' to-day to see me!
My best I've done for every one—
  My heart gets their caressing;
It seems to me like a Christmas tree,
  Hung round with every blessing.
(Of course I know that this all must
    go ;—
  But grief wasn't made to borrow,
And I'd get my pay for the fact
    to-day,
  If I knew I should die to-mor-
    row !)

[FARMER'S WIFE.]

Let's see—there'll be ten—eleven—twelve—on this side,
　　The old table's growing too small;
Our larder, as well as our hearts, must provide,
　　And our hearts will make room for them all.

There'll be Jim with his jokes (and I hope they'll be new,
　　Not those he has told twice before);
There'll be Sam with his stories, more startling than true,
　　Which always remind him of more;

There'll be Kate, with her fat little pig of a lad,
　　Whose stomach unceasingly begs;
And her other one, who, though not cut out for bad,
　　Is a hurricane mounted on legs;

There'll be John, with his tiny brown tribe of brunettes,
　　And Lue, with her one little blonde;
And Tom, with two armfuls of wife and their pets,
　　A trifle too startlingly fond!

For 'tis dangerous business—this loving too well—
　　It somehow brings Heaven over-near;
When our hearts their sweet stories too noisily tell,
　　The angels are certain to hear;

The angels are certain to hear what we say,
　　In their search for the brightest and best;
And they're likely to carry our prizes away,
　　To make Heaven more happy and blest.

Though our table be short, yet our hearts extend wide—
　　This food's with no stinginess chilled;
Let's see: there'll be ten—eleven—twelve—on this side—
　　And—the chair that will never be filled.

Oh my poor darling boy, lying silent to-day,
　　With the storm spading snow on your breast!

The angels, they found you, and made you their prey,
  In their search for the brightest and best!

My boy-love! I did not believe you would go!
  How I begged and implored you to wake,
As you lay here so white, on that dark day of woe,
  That they brought you home, drowned, from the lake!

And whoever may come, and whatever betide,
  You still have your room and your chair;
Is it true that I feel you sometimes at my side,
  And your lips on my forehead and hair?

The house will be running clear over with glee,
  We all shall be merry to-day;
But Christmas is never quite Christmas to me,
  With one of my loved ones away.

# THE FESTIVAL OF ANECDOTE;

OR,

## AN EVENING IN THE COUNTRY STORE.

## I.

An evening in the quaint old country store!
While Winter's feet were kicking at the door,
And Winter's white-nailed fingers striving hard
To raise the windows he himself had barred;
Save when he chased upon their weary rounds,
Through tracks of air, his yelling tempest-hounds.
Bark louder, storm-dogs! to our dreamy sight,
Your voices made the fire-cheer twice as bright,
Promoting high beyond a moment's doubt,
The value of the dry-goods shelved about.

There's little you'll be wanting, cheap or dear,
That has not something somewhat like it, here;
Whatever honest people drink or eat,
Or pack their bodies in, from head to feet,
Want what you may, you'll get it—search no more—
Or imitation of it—in this store.
The body's needs not only here you find,
But food, too, for the sympathies and mind;
For in one corner, fed by many lands,
The small post-office dignifiedly stands,
With square, red-numbered boxes in its arms,
Well stocked with white and brown enveloped charms.
Here the lithe girl, irresolutely gay,
Asks if there's "anything for us to-day";

"ASKS IF THERE'S 'ANY THING FOR US TO-DAY.'"

Here the farm lad, who wider fields would seek,
Comes for the county paper once a week.
Through this delivery port-hole there is hurled
Printed bombardment from the outside world;
The great, far world, whose heart-throbs, up and down,
Strike pulses, e'en within this quiet town.

The quaint, well populated country store!
A hospitable, mirth-productive shore,
Where masculine barks take refuge from distress,
In the port of an evening's cheerfulness.
The rusty stove, with wood-fed heat endowed,
Shoots hot invisible arrows at the crowd,
To which the chewing population nigh
Send back a prompt and vigorous reply,
And find time for side-battles of retort,
In various moralled stories, long and short:
From one that's smart and good enough to print,
To one that has a hundred hell-seeds in 't.
Here laws are put on trial by debate,
Here solved conundrums, both of Church and State;
Here is contested, with more voice than brain,
Full many a hot political campaign;
The half surmised shortcomings of the church
Are opened to some sinner's anxious search;
And criticisms the minister gets here,
From men who have not heard him once a year.
Or maybe some inside the sacred fold
No longer their experiences can hold
Within the flock, who 've harked to them so oft,
Invariably referring them aloft,
That, tired of this monotony, they yearn
A little godless sympathy to earn.
And maybe it is one of these, who now,
With elevated feet and earnest brow,
And face where sentiment flits to and fro,
Tells sorrows he has felt not long ago:

"AND HE STUDIED QUITE A LITTLE ERE HE GOT THE PROPER REFERENCE."

[ OUR TRAVELED PARSON. ]

For twenty years and over, our good parson had been toiling,
To chip the bad meat from our hearts, and keep the good from
     spoiling;
But suddenly he wilted down, and went to looking sickly,
And the doctor said that something must be put up for him quickly.
So we kind o' clubbed together, each according to his notion,
And bought a circular ticket, in the lands across the ocean;
Wrapped some pocket-money in it—what we thought would easy do
     him—
And appointed me committee-man, to go and take it to him.
I found him in his study, looking rather worse than ever;
And told him 'twas decided that his flock and he should sever.
Then his eyes grew big with wonder, and it seemed almost to blind 'em,
And some tears looked out o' window, with some others close behind 'em!
But I handed him the ticket, with a little bow of deference,
And he studied quite a little ere he got the proper reference;
And then the tears that waited—great unmanageable creatures—
Let themselves quite out o' window, and came climbing down his feat-
     ures.

I wish you could ha' seen him, when he came back, fresh and glow-
  ing,
His clothes all worn and seedy, and his face all fat and knowing;
I wish you could ha' heard him, when he prayed for us who sent him,
Paying back with compound int'rst every dollar that we'd lent him!
'Twas a feast to true believers—'twas a blight on contradiction—
To hear one just from Calvary talk about the crucifixion;
'Twas a damper on those fellows who pretended they could doubt it,
To have a man who'd been there stand and tell 'em all about it!
Why every foot of Scripture, whose location used to stump us,
Was now regularly laid out with the different points o' compass;
When he undertook a subject, in what nat'ral lines he'd draw it!
He would paint it out so honest that it seemed as if you saw it.
And the way he went for Europe! oh, the way he scampered through it!
Not a mountain but he clim' it—not a city but he knew it;
There wasn't any subject to explain, in all creation,
But he could go to Europe and bring back an illustration!
So we crowded out to hear him, quite instructed and delighted;
'Twas a picture-show, a lecture, and a sermon—all united;
And my wife would rub her glasses, and serenely pet her Test'ment,
And whisper, "That 'ere ticket was a splendid good investment."

Now, after six months' travel, we was most of us all ready
To settle down a little, so 's to live more staid and steady;
To develop home resources, with no foreign cares to fret us,
Using house-made faith more frequent; but our parson wouldn't let us!
To view the same old scenery, time and time again he'd call us—
Over rivers, plains, and mountains he would any minute haul us;
He slighted our soul-sorrows, and our spirits' aches and ailings,
To get the cargo ready for his regular Sunday sailings!
Why, he'd take us off a-touring, in all spiritual weather,
Till we at last got home-sick and sea-sick all together!
And "I wish to all that's peaceful," said one free-expressioned brother,
"That The Lord had made one cont'nent, an' then never made another!"

Sometimes, indeed, he'd take us into old, familiar places,
And pull along quite nat'ral, in the good old Gospel traces:
But soon my wife would shudder, just as if a chill had got her,
Whispering, "Oh, my goodness gracious! he's a-takin' to the water!"

And it wasn't the same old comfort, when he called around to see us;
On some branch of foreign travel he was sure at last to tree us;
All unconscious of his error, he would sweetly patronize us,
And with oft-repeated stories still endeavor to surprise us.

"'TWAS A PICTURE-SHOW, A LECTURE, AND A SERMON, ALL UNITED."

And the sinners got to laughing; and that fin'lly galled and stung us,
To ask him, Wouldn't he kindly once more settle down among us?
Didn't he think that more home produce would improve our soul's
    digestions?
They appointed me committee-man to go and ask the questions.
I found him in his garden, trim an' buoyant as a feather;
He shook my hand, exclaiming, "This is quite Italian weather!
How it 'minds me of the evenings when, your distant hearts caressing,
Upon my dear, good brothers, I invoked God's choicest blessing!"

"I FOUND HIM IN HIS GARDEN, TRIM AN' BUOYANT AS A FEATHER."

I went and told the brothers, "No; I can not bear to grieve him;
He's so happy in his exile, it's the proper place to leave him.
I took that journey to him, and right bitterly I rue it;
But I can not take it from him; if *you* want to, go and do it."

Now a new restraint entirely seemed next Sunday to enfold him,
And he looked so hurt and humbled, that I knew that they had told
    him.
Subdued-like was his manner, and some tones were hardly vocal;
But every word and sentence was pre-eminently local!

Still, the sermon sounded awkward, and we awkward felt who
    heard it;
'Twas a grief to see him steer it—'twas a pain to hear him word it.
"When I was abroad"—was maybe half a dozen times repeated,
But that sentence seemed to choke him, and was always uncompleted.

As weeks went on, his old smile would occasionally brighten,
But the voice was growing feeble, and the face began to whiten;
He would look off to the eastward, with a wistful, weary sighing,
And 'twas whispered that our pastor in a foreign land was dying.

The coffin lay 'mid garlands, smiling sad as if they knew us;
The patient face within it preached a final sermon to us;
Our parson *had* gone touring—on a trip he'd long been earning—
In that wonder-land, whence tickets are not issued for returning!
O tender, good heart-shepherd! your sweet smiling lips, half-parted,
Told of scenery that burst on you, just the minute that you started!
Could you preach once more among us, you might wander, without
    fearing;
You could give us tales of glory that we'd never tire of hearing!

## II.

The grave sends fascination with its fear:
We shrink and dread to see it yawning near,
But when on others falls the endless spell,
We like to talk about it mighty well;
And handle o'er, with fear-abated breath,
The gruesome, grim particulars of death.
Never can horror so a tale unfold,
But curious mortals love to hear it told,
As if they were not of the race they view,
And subject to the same conditions, too.
When the last speaker had a period found,
And placed his parson safely under-ground,
Mortality of every phase and age
Became at once the conversational rage;
And he was sachem of our gossip-tribe,
Who had the dolefulest death-pangs to describe.

Most well I recollect, of course (though least),
My own addition to the horror-feast.
I had seen two men hanged, for some red crime
Committed in drink's murder-harvest time;
By sheriff-usher through the jail-yard shown,
They walked unto this funeral of their own;
Their rites were said by one in priesthood's guise:
Two empty coffins lay before their eyes.
One scarcely yet had left youth's pleasure-vale;
(His mother waited for him near the jail.)
The other had his tutor been in crime,
And sold the devil half a manhood's time.
They did not flinch, when first frowned on their sight
Their gallows death-bed, standing bolt-upright:
But when the youngster turned and took his place,
A cold wind brushed the noose against his face;
Then first that feigned indifference seemed to fail;
Death, when it came, made not the boy more pale.
(I saw him in the coffin, after this;
It was a face that woman-eyes would kiss.)
Close to his side, notice the older pass:
Teacher and pupil, standing in one class.
This rogue had learned a knack to calmly die,
And glanced the younger wretch a cold good-bye;
But he, unmagnetized from past control,
With silent-moving lips prayed for his soul.
(The black cap hid the last part of his prayer,
And shut it in, but could not keep it there.)
He had prayed for his body, had he known;
For while the older died without a groan,
When with a "thud!" the two went bounding high,
He struggled, gasped, and wailed, but could not die,
Till the slow-gripping rope had choked him quite,
And strong men fainted at the piteous sight.
(I thought I told this pretty middling well;
But was eclipsed by an old sea-dog swell,
Anchored by age in our calm rustic bay,
Who'd seen twelve Turks beheaded in one day.)

Then followed accidents, by field and flood,
Such as had fettered breath or loosened blood;
Fires, earthquakes, shipwrecks, and such cheerful themes,
Furnished material for our future dreams.
And when at last there came a little pause
(The silent horror-method of applause),
A lad, with face appropriately long,
Said, "Jacob, won't you sing that little song
That you sat up all t'other night to make,
About the children drownded in the lake?"
Jacob, whose efforts none had need to urge,
Promptly materialized the following dirge:


### [A DIRGE OF THE LAKE.]

On the lake—on the lake—
    The sun the day is tingeing;
The sky's rich hue shows brighter blue
    Above its forest fringing.
The breezes high blow far and nigh
    White cloudlets, like a feather;
The breezes low sweep to and fro,
    And wavelets race together.

Up the lake—up the lake—
    The busy oars are dipping;
The blades of wood that cleave the flood,
    With streamlets fresh are dripping.
A graceful throng of golden song
    Comes floating smoothly after;
Like silver chains, ring loud the strains
    Of childhood's merry laughter.

By the lake—by the lake—
    The lilies' heads are lifting,
And into night the warmth and light
    Of happy homes are drifting.
The bright sun-rays upon them gaze,
    In pity unavailing;

With laughing eyes, between two skies
  They for the grave are sailing.

In the lake—in the lake—
  The barge is sinking steady;
A startled hush, a frantic rush—
  The feast of Death is ready!
A pleading cry, a faint reply,
  A frenzied, brave endeavor—
And o'er them deep the wavelets creep,
  And smile as sweet as ever.

'Neath the lake—'neath the lake—
  The wearied forms are lying;
They sleep away their gala-day—
  Too fair a day for dying!
With hands that grasped, and nothing clasped,
  With terror-frozen faces,
In slimy caves and gloomy graves,
  They nestle to their places.

From the lake—from the lake—
  They one by one are creeping;
Their very rest is grief-possessed,
  And piteous looks their sleeping.
Upon no face is any trace
  Of sickness' friendly warning,
But sad they lie 'neath even-sky,
  Who were so gay at morning!

O'er the lake—o'er the lake—
  A spectre bark is sailing;
There is no cry of danger nigh,
  There is no sound of wailing.
They who have died gaze from its side—
  Their spirit-faces glowing;
For through the skies the life-boat plies,
  And angel hands are rowing.

## III.

There was among our various-tempered crowd,
A graduate; who, having last year plowed
The utmost furrow of scholastic lore,
Now boarded with his father, as before.
His course was hard, but he had mastered all:
Aquatics, billiards, flirting, and base-ball;
And now, once more to rural science turned,
Was leisurely unlearning what he'd learned.
The death-theme made him sad and serious-eyed,
About a college comrade who had died;
And with a sudden, strong sigh-lengthened breath,
He gave this boyish paragraph of death:


[THE DEAD STUDENT.]

'Twas mighty slow to make it seem as if poor Brown was dead;
'Twas only just the day he died, he had to take his bed;
The day before, he played first-base, and ran McFarland down;
And then to slip away so sly—'twas not at all like Brown.

'Twas hard for my own life to leave that fellow's life behind;
'Tis work, sometimes, to get a man well laid out in your mind!
It wouldn't have shook me very much, long after all was o'er,
To hear a whoop, and see the man go rushing past my door!

Poor Brown!—so white and newly still within his room he lay!
I called upon him, as it were, at noon the second day.
A-rushing into Brownie's room seemed awkward-like, and queer;
We hadn't spoken back and forth for something like a year.

We never pulled together square a single night or day:
Whate'er direction I might start, Brown went the other way;
(Excepting in our love affairs; we picked a dozen bones
About a girl Smith tried to get, who fin'lly married Jones.)

He worked against me in our class, before my very eyes;
He opened up and scooped me square out of the Junior prize;

I never wanted any place, clean from the last to first,
But Brown was sure to have a friend who wanted it the worst;

In the last campus rush, we came to strictly business blows,
And with the eye he left undimmed, I viewed his damaged nose;
In short, I came at last to feel—I own it with dismay—
That life would be worth living for, if Brown were out the way.

"I CALLED UPON HIM, AS IT WERE, AT NOON THE SECOND DAY."

He lay within his dingy room, as white as drifted snow—
Things all around were wondrous neat—the women fixed them so;
'Twas plain he had no hand in that, and naught about it knew;
To 've seen the order lying round, it would have made him blue!

A bright bouquet of girlish flowers smiled on the scene of death,
And through the open window came a sweet geranium-breath;

Close-caged, a small canary bird, with glossy, yellow throat,
Tripped drearily from perch to perch, and never sung a note;

With hair unusually combed, sat poor McFarland near,
Alternately perusing Greek, and wrestling with a tear;
A homely little girl of six, for some old kindness' sake,
Sat sobbing in a corner near, as if her heart would break;

The books looked pale and wretched-like, almost as if they knew,
And seemed to be a-whispering their titles to the view;
His rod and gun were in their place; and high where all could see,
Gleamed jauntily the boating-cup he won last year from me;

I lifted up the solemn sheet; the honest, manly face
Had signs of study and of toil that death could not erase;
As western skies at twilight mark where late the sun has been,
Brown's face showed yet the mind and soul that late had burned within

He looked so grandly helpless there upon that lonely bed—
Ah me! these manly foes are foes no more when they are dead!
" Old boy," said I, " 'twas half my fault; this heart makes late amends."
I grasped the white cold hand in mine—and Brown and I were friends.

### IV.

"That was a sudden death, 'twill be allowed,"
Said a half-Yankeed Scotchman in the crowd:
"We never know what paths may help or kill;
Death has a-many ways to work his will.
It is his daily study and his care,
To utilize earth, water, fire, and air,
Seduce them from their master man's employ,
And make the traitors murder and destroy.
Men call this "accident." Of one I know,
That came about not very long ago,
Where I once lived, three thousand miles away;
I read it in my paper, yesterday."
Then, with a strong voice that came not amiss,
He told the story, something like to this:

[THE DEATH-BRIDGE OF THE TAY.]

The night and the storm fell together upon the old town of Dundee,
And, trembling, the mighty firth-river held out its cold hand toward
    the sea.
Like the dull-booming bolts of a cannon, the wind swept the streets
    and the shores;
It wrenched at the roofs and the chimneys—it crashed 'gainst the win-
    dows and doors;
Like a mob that is drunken and frenzied, it surged through the streets
    up and down,
And screamed the sharp, shrill cry of "Murder!" o'er river and hill-top
    and town.
It leaned its great breast 'gainst the belfries—it perched upon minaret
    and dome—
Then sprang on the shivering firth-river, and tortured its waves into
    foam.
'Twas a night when the landsman seeks shelter, and cares not to ven-
    ture abroad;
When the sailor clings close to the rigging, and prays for the mercy
    of God.

Look! the moon has come out, clad in splendor, the turbulent scene to
    behold;
She smiles at the night's devastation—she dresses the storm-king in gold.
She kindles the air with her cold flame, as if to her hand it were given
To light the frail earth to its ruin, with the tenderest radiance of
    heaven.
Away to the north, ragged mountains climb high through the shud-
    dering air;
They bend their dark brows o'er the valley, to read what new ruin is
    there.
Along the shore-line creeps the city, in crouching and sinuous shape,
With firesides so soon to be darkened, and doors to be shaded with
    crape!
To the south, like a spider-web waving, there curves, for a two-mile
    away,
This world's latest man-devised wonder—the far-famed bridge of the
    Tay.

It stretches and gleams into distance; it creeps the broad stream o'er
   and o'er,
Till it rests its strong, delicate fingers in the palm of the opposite
   shore.
But look! through the mists of the southward, there flash to the eye,
   clear and plain,
Like a meteor that's bound to destruction—the lights of a swift-coming
   train!

O cruel and bloodthirsty tempest! we sons of humanity know,
Wherever and whene'er we find you, that you are our faithfulest foe!
You plow with the death-pointed cyclone wherever life's dwellings
   may be;
You spur your fire-steeds through our cities—you scuttle our ships on
   the sea.
The storm-shaken sailor has cursed you; white hands have implored
   you in vain;
And still you have filled Death's dominions, and laughed at humanity's
   pain.
But ne'er in the cave where your dark deeds are plotted and hid from
   the light,
Was one half so cruel and treacherous as this you have kept for to-
   night!
You lurked 'round this bridge in its building; you counted each span
   and each pier;
You marked the men's daily endeavors — you looked at them all with
   a sneer;
You laughed at the brain-girded structure; you deemed it an easy-
   fought foe,
And bided the time when its builders your easy-plied prowess should
   know.
O tempest! feed full with destruction! fling down these iron beams
   from on high!
But temper your triumph with mercy, and wait till the train has
   gone by!

O angels! sweet guardian angels!—who once in the body drew breath,
Till, wearied, you found the great river, and crossed on the black bridge
   of death,

You who, from the shores of the sun-land, fly back on the wings of
    the soul,
And round your frail earth-loves yet hover, and strive their weak steps
    to control,
Look out through the mists to the southward!—the hearts on yon swift-
    coming train,
So light and so happy this moment, are rushing to terror and pain!
Oh whisper a word to the driver, that till morning the bridge be not
    braved;
At the cost of a night lost in waiting, the years of these lives may be
    saved!
On yon cheer-freighted train there are hundreds, who soon beyond
    help will be hurled;
Oh whisper to them the dread secret, before it is known to the
    world!
On this home-lighted shore are full many who wait for their friends,
    blithe and gay;
They will wait through full many a night-time—through many a sor-
    row-strewn day.
The trim evening lamps from the windows their comfort-charged beau-
    ty will shed;
The fire will burn bright on the hearth-stone—its rays will be cheer-
    ful and red;
The sun will come out of the cold sea—the morning will rise clear
    and bright,
But death will eclipse all its radiance, and darken your world into
    night!

'Mid the lights that so gayly are gleaming yon city of Dundee
    within,
Is one that is waiting a wanderer, who long o'er the ocean has been.
His age-burdened parents are watching from the window that looks on
    the firth,
For the train that will come with their darling—their truest-loved
    treasure on earth.
"He'll be comin' the nicht," says the father, "for sure the hand-writ-
    in's his ain;
The letter says, 'Ha' the lamp lichted—I'll come on the seven o'clock
    train.
             6

For years in the mines I've been toiling, in this wonderfu' West, o'er
the sea;
My work has brought back kingly wages — there's plenty for you an'
for me.
Your last days shall e'en be your best days; the high-stepping young-
ster you knew,
Who cost so much care in his raising, now 'll care for himself and for
you.
Gang not to the station to meet me; ye never need run for me more;
But when ye shall hear the gate clickit, ye maun rise up an' open the
door.
We will hae the first glow of our greeting when nae one o' strangers
be nigh,
We will smile out the joy o' our meeting on the spot where we wept
our good-bye.
Ye maun put me a plate on the table, an' set in the auld place a
chair;
An' if but the good Lord be willing, doubt never a bit I'll be there.
So sit ye an' wait for my coming (ye will na' watch for me in vain),
An' see me glide over the river, along o' the roar o' the train.
Ye may sit at the southernmost window, for I will come hame from
that way;
I will fly where I swam, when a youngster, across the broad Firth o'
the Tay.' "


So they sit at the southernmost window, the parents, with hand clasped
in hand,
And gaze o'er the tempest - vexed waters, across to the storm - shaken
land.
They see the bold acrobat-monster creep out on the treacherous line;
Its cinder-breath glitters like star-dust—its lamp-eyes they glimmer and
shine.
It braces itself 'gainst the tempest — it fights for each inch with the
foe—
With torrents of air all around it—with torrents of water below.
But look! look! the monster is stumbling, while trembles the fragile
bridge-wall—
They struggle like athletes entwining — then both like a thunder - bolt
fall!

"BUT LOOK! LOOK! THE MONSTER IS STUMBLING!"

Down, down through the dark the train plunges, with speed unaccustomed and dire;

It glows with its last dying beauty — it gleams like a hail-storm of fire!

No wonder the mother faints death-like, and clings like a clod to the floor;

No wonder the man flies in frenzy, and dashes his way through the door!

He fights his way out through the tempest; he is beaten and baffled and tossed;

He cries, "*The train's gang off the Tay brig! lend help here to look for the lost!*"

Oh, little to him do they listen, the crowds to the river that flee;

The news, like the shock of an earthquake, has thrilled through the town of Dundee.

Like travelers belated, they're rushing to where the bare station-walls frown;

Suspense twists the blade of their anguish—like maniacs they run up and down.

Out, out, creep two brave, sturdy fellows, o'er danger-strewn buttress and piers;

They can climb 'gainst that blast, for they carry the blood of old Scotch mountaineers.

But they leave it along as they clamber; they mark all their hand-path with red;

Till they come where the torrent leaps bridgeless—a grave dancing over its dead.

A moment they gaze down in horror; then creep from the death-laden tide,

With the news, "There's nae help for our loved ones, save God's mercy for them who have died!"

How sweetly the sunlight can sparkle o'er graves where our best hopes have lain!

How brightly its gold beams can glisten on faces that whiten with pain!

Oh, never more gay were the wavelets, and careless in innocent glee,

And never more sweet did the sunrise shine over the town of Dundee.

"OUT, OUT, CREEP TWO BRAVE, STURDY FELLOWS."

But though the town welcomed the morning, and the firth threw its
    gold lances back,
On the hearts of the grief-stricken people death's cloud rested heavy
    and black.
And the couple who waited last evening their man-statured son to
    accost,
Now laid their heads down on the table, and mourned for the boy
    that was lost.
"'Twas sae sad," moaned the crushed, aged mother, each word dripping
    o'er with a tear,
"Sae far he should come for to find us, and then he should perish sae
    near!
O Robin, my bairn! ye did wander far from us for mony a day,
And when ye ha' come back sae near us, why could na' ye come a' the
    way?"

"I *hae* come a' the way," said a strong voice, and a bearded and
    sun-beaten face

Smiled on them the first joyous pressure of one long and filial em-
    brace:

"I cam' on last nicht far as Newport; but Maggie, my bride that's to
    be,

She ran through the storm to the station, to get the first greeting o'
    me.

I leaped from the carriage to kiss her; she held me sae fast and sae
    ticht,

The train it ran off and did leave me; I could na' get over the nicht.

I tried for to walk the brig over—my head it was a' in a whirl—

I could na'—ye know the sad reason—I had to go back to my girl!

I hope ye'll tak' kindly to Maggie; she's promised to soon be my
    wife;

She's a darling wee bit of a lassie, and her fondness it saved me my
    life."


The night and the storm fell together upon the sad town of Dundee,

The half-smothered song of the tempest swept out like a sob to the
    sea;

The voice of the treacherous storm-king, as mourning for them he had
    slain;

O cruel and blood-thirsty tempest! your false tears are shed all in
    vain!

Beneath the dread roof of this ruin your sad victims nestle and creep;

They hear not the voices that call them; if they come, they will come
    in their sleep.

No word can they tell of their terror, no step of the dark route re-
    trace,

Unless their sad story be written upon the white page of the face.

Perchance *that* may speak of their anguish when first came the crash
    of despair;

The long-drawn suspense of the instant they plunged through the
    shuddering air;

The life-panoramas that flitted swift past them, with duties undone;

The brave fight for life in a battle that strong death already had won;

The half stifled shouting of anguish the aid of high Heaven to implore;

The last patient pang of submission, when effort was ended and o'er.

"SHE HELD ME SAE FAST AND SAE TICHT."

But, tempest, a bright star in heaven a message of comfort sends
    back,
And draws our dim glances to skyward, away from thy laurels of
    black:
Thank God that whatever the darkness that covers his creature's dim
    sight,
He always vouchsafes *some* deliverance, throws *some one* a sweet ray of
    light;
Thank God that the strength of his goodness from dark depths ascended
    on high,
And carried the souls of the suffering away to the realms of the sky;

Thank God that his well-tempered mercy came down with the clouds
    from above,
And saved one from out the destruction, and him by the angel of love.


## V.

What mind-smith who can trace the subtle links
That join a man's ideas, when he thinks?
Given the thought by which he's pleased or vexed,
Who can predict what one will strike him next?
Given a memory, who can tell us all
The other memories that its voice may call?
Given a fancy, who betimes can read
What other unlike fancies it may breed?
Given a fact, who surely can foreknow
What distant relatives may come and go?
Beneath our thoughts, thoughts hidden thickly teem;
Each mind is but a stream above a stream.
Given a story, what dissimilar one
May 't not remind you of before 'tis done!
Scarce had the Scotchman's tale been fairly told,
When a quaint farmer, wrinkled but not old,
Hastened to execute a cross-leg change,
And with no consciousness of seeming strange,
Leaped from the thought-depths that had him immersed,
His conversational puff-ball sharply burst,
Contributing, with countenance severe,
These notes, from his pecuniary career,
As if the average listener it might strike,
That the two tales were sing'larly alike:


### [THE LIGHTNING-ROD DISPENSER.]

Which this railroad smash reminds me, in an underhanded way,
Of a lightning-rod dispenser that came down on me one day;
Oiled to order in his motions—sanctimonious in his mien—
Hands as white as any baby's, an' a face unnat'ral clean;
Not a wrinkle had his raiment, teeth and linen glittered white,
And his new-constructed neck-tie was an interestin' sight!

Which I almost wish a razor had made red that white-skinned throat,
And that new-constructed neck-tie had composed a hangman's knot,
Ere he brought his sleek-trimmed carcass for my woman-folks to
　　see,
And his buzz-saw tongue a-runnin' for to gouge a gash in me!

Still I couldn't help but like him—as I fear I al'ays must,
The gold o' my own doctrines in a fellow-heap o' dust;
For I saw that my opinions, when I fired 'em round by round,
Brought back an answerin' volley of a mighty similar sound.
I touched him on religion, and the joys my heart had known:
And I found that he had very similar notions of his own!
I told him of the doubtings that made sad my boyhood years:
Why, he'd laid awake till morning with that same old breed of fears!
I pointed up the pathway that I hoped to Heaven to go:
He was on that very ladder, only just a round below!
Our politics was different, and at first he galled and winced;
But I arg'ed him so able, he was very soon convinced.

And 'twas gettin' tow'rd the middle of a hungry Summer day—
There was dinner on the table, and I asked him, would he stay?
And he sat him down among us—everlastin' trim and neat—
And he asked a short crisp blessin' almost good enough to eat!
Then he fired up on the mercies of our Everlastin' Friend,
Till he gi'n The Lord Almighty a good first-class recommend;
And for full an hour we listened to that sugar-coated scamp—
Talkin' like a blesséd angel—eatin' like a blasted tramp!

My wife—she liked the stranger, smiling on him, warm and sweet;
(It al'ays flatters women when their guests are on the eat!)
And he hinted that some ladies never lose their youthful charms,
And caressed her yearlin' baby, an' received it in his arms.
My sons and daughters liked him—for he had progressive views,
And he chewed the cud o' fancy, and gi'n down the latest news;
And *I* couldn't help but like him—as I fear I al'ays must,
The gold of my own doctrines in a fellow-heap o' dust.

He was chiselin' desolation through a piece of apple-pie,
When he paused an' gazed upon us, with a tear in his off-eye,

And said, "Oh happy family!—your joys they make me sad!
They all the time remind me of the dear ones once *I* had!
A babe as sweet as this one; a wife *almost* as fair;
A little girl with ringlets—like that one over there.
But had I not neglected the means within my way,
Then they might still be living, and loving me to-day.

"One night there came a tempest; the thunder-peals were dire;
The clouds that marched above us were shooting bolts of fire;
In my own house I lying, was thinking, to my blame,
How little I had guarded against those bolts of flame,
When crash!—through roof and ceiling the deadly lightning cleft,
And killed my wife and children, and only I was left!

"Since then afar I've wandered, and naught for life have cared,
Save to save others' loved ones whose lives have yet been spared;
Since then, it is my mission, where'er by sorrow tossed,
To sell to worthy people good lightning-rods at cost.
With sure and strong protection I'll clothe your buildings o'er;
'Twill cost you—twenty dollars (*perhaps* a *trifle* more;
Whatever else it comes to, at lowest price I'll put;
You simply *sign a contract* to pay so much per foot)."

I—signed it! while my family, all approvin', stood about;
The villain dropped a tear on 't—but he didn't blot it out!
That self-same day, with wagons came some rascals great and small;
They hopped up on my buildin's just as if they owned 'em all;
They hewed 'em and they hacked 'em—ag'in' my loud desires—
They trimmed 'em off with gewgaws, and they bound 'em down with wires;
They hacked 'em and they hewed 'em, and they hewed and hacked 'em
    still,
And every precious minute kep' a runnin' up the bill.

To find my soft-spoke neighbor, did I rave and rush an' run:
He was suppin' with a neighbor, just a few miles further on.
"Do you think," I loudly shouted, "that I need a mile o' wire,
For to save each separate hay-cock out o' heaven's consumin' fire?
Did you think, to keep my buildin's out o' some uncertain harm,
I was goin' to deed you over all the balance of my farm?"

"'TWAS THE VERY FIRST OCCASION HE HAD DISAGREED WITH ME!"

He silenced me with silence in a very little while,
And then trotted out the contract with a reassuring smile;
And for half an hour explained it, with exasperatin' skill,
While his myrmurdums kep' probably a-runnin' up my bill.
He held me to that contract with a firmness queer to see;
'Twas the very first occasion he had disagreed with me!
And for that 'ere thunder story, ere the rascal finally went,
I paid two hundred dollars, if I paid a single cent.

And if any lightnin'-rodist wants a dinner-dialogue
With the restaurant department of an enterprisin' dog,

Let him set his mouth a-runnin', just inside my outside gate;
And I'll bet two hundred dollars that he don't have long to wait.

## VI.

"Time to shut up," the lean store-keeper said:
"It's time that honest folks should be in bed.
And all this crowd I honest hold to be,
And penniless, so far as I can see;
If there's a cent here, it's well out of sight;
My cash-box has not seen it; friends, good-night!"

# THE FESTIVAL OF CLAMOR;

OR,

## THE TOWN MEETING.

'Twas our regular annual town-meeting;
    And smooth as a saint could desire,
Our work we were swiftly completing,
    Till it came to electing a "Squire";

Which office retained a slight vestige
    Of old country power, as it were,
And most of the honor and prestige
    A township like ours could confer.

Which office (with latitude speaking),
    Commencing nobody knew when,
Had long been relentlessly seeking
    Two very respectable men;

For in virtuous political cases,
    'Tis known as the regular plan,
That the man must not seek for the places;
    The places must seek for the man.

But past these two men, and around them,
    The squireship had happened to roam,
And, strangely, had never yet found them,
    Although they were always at home;

And manfully laid fear behind them;
    And whispered to friends far and wide,
That if office was anxious to find them,
    They never were going to hide!

And now, in undignified action,
    Themselves and their partisans fought,
To decide, to their own satisfaction,
    Which one 'twas the office had sought.

A half day we clamored and voted,
    And each to success drew him nigh,
But neither as victor was quoted:
    It always resulted "a tie;"

All voted for one or the other;
    Except two young barbarous elves,
Who, simply proceedings to bother,
    Kept voting, like sin, for themselves;

(Except a few times, it was noted,
    Some charges of self-love to smother,
A conf'rence they had, ere they voted,
    Then proceeded to "go" for each other!)

So all of our voting and prating,
    To neither side victory brought,
While the office stood patiently waiting
    To find out which one it had sought.

Till, tired of these semi-reverses,
    A few of the worst of each clan
Loaded up their word-guns with sly curses,
    And fired at the opposite man.

And morally petrified wretches,
    These two men to be were allowed,
In small biographical sketches
    That began to appear in the crowd.

The one, as a swindler high-handed,
    Was painted unpleasantly plain;
With pockets like bladders expanded,
    And filled with unstatesman-like gain;

They stated that all his life-labors
  Were tinged with pecuniary sin;
That things left out nights by his neighbors,
  They frequently failed to take in;

"A HALF DAY WE CLAMORED AND VOTED."

They claimed that his business transactions
  Flowered out at the people's expense;
And named, as among these subtractions,
  Three dollars and twenty-nine cents.

No odds that he stoutly denied it—
    It hushed not the clamor at all;
Yet all the more fiercely they cried it,
    And chalked the amount on the wall.

And a letter was found that convicted
    This man to have some time been led
To have some time somehow contradicted
    Some things that he some time had said.

But really, until very recent,
    His name had not been a bad word;
*But naught he had done that was decent,*
    *To the minds of his foes now occurred.*

His nature was kindly intentioned,
    And free from ungenerous taint;
*A fact not obtrusively mentioned,*
    *In his enemies' bill of complaint.*

He rose from a low, humble station;
    His boy-life was sturdy and good;
He was hard-striving youth's inspiration;
    *They kept that as still as they could.*

He had sown gold successes for others;
    He cast a kind glance upon all;
No true men but what were his brothers;
    *They did not chalk that on the wall.*

He was cultured, and broad, and discerning;
    Strong thoughts on his countenance sat;
He dwelt by the fountains of learning;
    *They never accused him of that.*

In short, had he heard the malicious
    Black words that were throttling his cause,
He'd have shuddered to learn what a vicious
    Unholy old villain he was;

7

And, terms theological using,
    He e'en might have wished he were dead,
Had not the same linguistic bruising
    Adorned his antagonist's head.

They said *he* was haughty in greeting;
    Above all his neighbors he felt,
And to make him look slender in meeting,
    Wore under his jacket a belt;

That he always had hoped and expected
    The place he now openly sought,
But knew not enough, if elected,
    The office to fill as he ought;

That he just hummed the ancient tune "Tariff,"
    When other folks shouted and sang;
That he once had the luck to be sheriff,
    When a woman was sentenced to hang;

That his mind he had long been diverting
    With future political fame,
His head in a barrel inserting,
    And shouting out "Squire" to his name:

And while, like a ball, the words bounded,
    And doubled themselves, o'er and o'er,
He pondered how pompous it sounded,
    And went on and did it some more;

And that this rather terse conversation,
    And having been oft at it caught,
Comprised all the qualification
    He had for the office he sought.

Now his life had the grim, noble beauty
    The deed-painter's brush loves to tell;
He was one who had studied his duty,
    And done it exceedingly well;

He was one of the bravest and quickest
    To shield threatened Liberty's form ;
He stood where the bullets were thickest,
    To cover her safe from the storm ;

Well framed for his foes' admiration—
    Well-named by his friends " The Superb " ;
A part of the edge of the nation—
    His whole life a transitive verb ;—

He was worthy and grand—who could doubt it ?
    His fame was as fresh as the morn ;
*But his foemen forgot all about it,*
    *And drabbled his name with their scorn.*

No odds how turned out the election,
    Concerning the lesson I'd teach ;
But my conscience that night, on reflection,
    Made me this political speech :

" 'Tis over high time you repented,
    You servile young partisan hound,
For being to-day represented
    In that idiot asylum of sound !

" Henceforth, in these conflicts exciting,
    Learn, whether by speech or by pen,
With *principle's* sword to be fighting,
    And not to be slandering *men.*"

# THE FESTIVAL OF MELODY;

OR,

## THE SINGING-SCHOOL.

MR. ABRAHAM BATES was a tune-stricken man,
Built on an exclusively musical plan;
With a body and soul that with naught could commune,
Unless it might somehow be set to a tune.
His features, harmoniously solemn and grim,
Resembled a doleful old long-meter hymn;
His smile, half-obtrusively gentle and calm,
Suggested the livelier notes of a psalm;
And his form had a power the appearance to lend
Of an overgrown tuning-fork, set upon end.
They who his accomplishments fathomed, averred
That he knew every tune that he ever had heard;
And his wife had a secret we all helped her keep,
That he frequently snored a rough tune in his sleep.
When he walked through the fields, with an inward-turned ear,
And a general impression that no one was near,
He with forefinger stretched to its fullest command,
Would beat quadruple time on the palm of his hand
(So firmly his singing-school habits would cling),
With his "Down, left, right, up! down, left, right, up!  Sing!"

What a monarch he was, to us tune-killing wights,
When he stood in the school-house, on long Winter nights,
With a dignity born our young souls to o'erwhelm,
Proclaiming the laws of his musical realm!
The black-board behind him frowned fierce on our sight,
Its old forehead creased with five wrinkles of white,

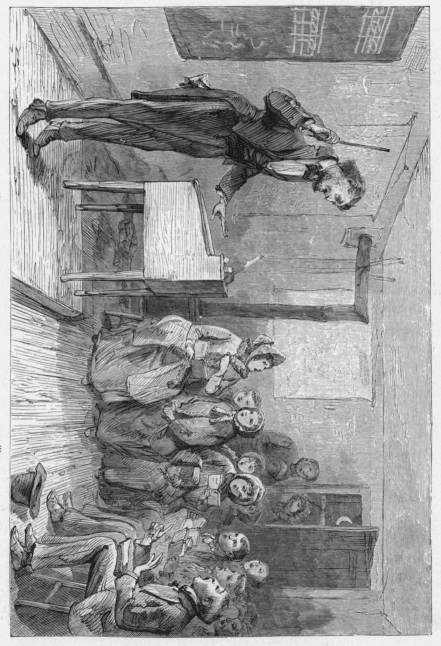

"WHAT A MONARCH HE WAS, TO US TUNE-KILLING WIGHTS!"

On which he paraded his armies of notes,
And sent on a raid through our eyes to our throats;
From the scenes of which partly harmonious turmoils
They issued, head-first, with our breath as their spoils.
How (in his particular specialty) grand
He looked, as he tiptoed, with bâton in hand,
And up, down, and up, in appropriate time,
Compelled us that slippery ladder to climb,
As he flourished his weapon, and marched to and fro,
With his "Do, re, mi, fa, sol, la, sol, la, si, do !"

Nathaniel F. Jennings! how sadly you tried,
With your eyes a third closed, and your mouth opened wide,
To sport an acceptable voice, like the rest,
And cultivate powers that you never possessed !
They were just out of music, it used to be said,
When they drafted the plan of your square, shaggy head.
You fired at each note, as it were, in the dark,
As an amateur rifleman would at a mark;
And short of opinion, till after the shot,
Of whether you'd happen to hit it or not.
E'en then you didn't know, till your sharp eye was told
By the way that the master's would flatter or scold.
The latter more oft; for your chances, sad wight,
Were seven to be wrong against one to be right,
And ne'er was a tune so mellifluously choice,
You could not embitter the same, with your voice.
But though your grim head hadn't the shade of a tone,
Your heart had a musical style of its own;
And we all found it out, 'neath the forest-trees wild,
The last night we hunted for Davis's child.
"May as well give it up," said our leader: "No good;
We've hunted three days and three nights in this wood;
We may as well look at it just as it is:
He's eaten or starved, long enough before this."
And Davis spoke up: "It's a fact, boys; he's right";
But he leaned 'gainst a tree, looking death-like and white.
*You* exclaimed, when your eyes his mute agony met.
"I'll be blanked if I'll stand this! I'll hunt a week yet !"

Poor Davis crept round till he got by your side,
Caught hold of your hand like a baby, and cried,
A picture of grateful, incompetent woe—
('Twas rather dramatic, as incidents go;)
Then we all of us yelled, in a magnetized cry,
An absurd proposition to find him, or die.
It was only an hour and a quarter from then
Your wing-shout came skurrying o'er woodland and glen,
As if to go round the whole world it would strive,
"I've found the young blank, an' he's here an' alive!"
Your voice had, as usual, less music than might,
But you led a remarkable chorus that night;
An anthem of joy swelled from many a throat,
And you, as our chorister, gave the first note.
When your hand was near squeezed out of shape by your mates,
None shook it more warmly than Abraham Bates;
Who, suggesting (to you) an impossible thing,
Shouted, "Down, up! down, up!   Sing!"

Little Clarissa Smith! how you thrilled through us all,
When you made that young soul-sweetened voice rise and fall!
The whippoorwill's voice is sweet-spoken and true,
But not with a heart and a spirit like you;
The lark trails the music of earth through the skies,
But the flame of her song does not flash from her eyes!
Our girl prima-donna!—Your fame was not spread,
Nor by world-wide applauses your vanity fed;
But you star with a grand brilliant company, now:
The laurels of Heaven have encircled your brow.
'Twas a dreary procession you led on that day
When so still in the old-fashioned coffin you lay;
No delicate casket, grief-laden with care,
And trimmed with exotics expensive and rare,
Had ever more tears on its occupant shed
Than you, in your old-fashioned coffin of red.
'Twas strange how the unstudied wiles of your art
Had soothed and delighted the average heart;
How much of Heaven's glory had glittered and smiled
Through the cultureless voice of an innocent child.

You looked very pretty, and half saucy, there,
With natural flowers in your girlish-combed hair;
And a little old half-worn-out book on your breast,
Containing the hymns that you used to sing best.
The roughest old villain that lived in our town
Stood back from the grave, and, with head hanging down,
Was heard, in a reverent whisper, to say,
"Heaven needed that voice, and God took it away."
And Abraham Bates, who, 'twas general belief,
Had never before given rein to a grief,
Felt sorrow sweep over his heart like a storm,
When it came, as it were, in a musical form;
And choked down and sobbed, with eyes filled to the brim,
While attempting to lead in the funeral hymn.
And long when the sound of that sorrow had waned,
In his rough old heart-caverns its echo remained;
And audible tears to the surface would spring,
Of that "Down, left, up! down, left, up! Sing!"

Mrs. Caroline Dean, how *you* revelled in song!
There was no singing-school to which you didn't belong,
Save in some locality far away, so
That you and your meek little husband couldn't go.
What a method was yours, of appearing prepared
To make every tune in the note-book look scared!
Your voice was voluminous, rather than rich,
And not predistinguished for accurate pitch;
But you seemed every word to o'erpoweringly feel,
And humbled and drove away skill with your zeal.
The villain referred to above, on the day
That you and your larynx were safe stowed away,
Didn't make the remark he was credited with
At the time of the burial of Clarissa Smith,
But muttered, as low with himself he communed,
"I suppose she will do, when they get her retuned."
Though the strains of the choir sounded weak and afraid
Without your soprano's stentorian aid,
Mr. Abraham Bates, if I was not deceived,
Worked lighter in harness, and acted relieved;

And when the hymn stated you "lovely and mild,"
And "as summer breeze gentle," he very near smiled;
For those who had learned his biography, knew
He had rather encounter a tempest than you,
When he dared, with a placating, angular smile.
To venture a hint on your musical style.
You remember how promptly he wilted, among
The tropical rays of your scorn-blazing tongue;
For your talents you easily turned, when you chose,
From fancy-gemmed song into plain business prose.
You knew how to make him as miserably meek
As a tin-peddler's horse at the close of the week.
You knew how to make a most desperate thing
That " Down, left, right, up!   Sing !"

Sweet hymn-tunes of old !—You had blood in your hearts,
That pulsed glowing life through your several parts:
From bass to soprano it surgingly climbed,
As grandly the chords of your melody chimed !
"Coronation," that brought royal splendors in view,
And solemn " Old Hundred," invariably new—
That golden sledge-hammer, of ponderous grace,
That drove every word like a wedge to its place;
" Balerma," of melody full to the brim,
And "Pleyel's" grandly plaintive melodious hymn;
With others, that memory's ear loves to greet,
Which, with different names, might have sounded less sweet.
Then with what a loud concatenation of sounds
We charged in our might on the glees and the rounds !
There was nothing, though polished, or harsh and unkempt,
That we had not courage enough to attempt;
And if tunes, when suggestion of murder arrives,
Were not gifted, like cats, with a number of lives,
There's many a living and healthy old strain,
We'd have sent long ago to repose with the slain.

O strong Winter nights ! when all earth was aglow
With crystal stars dancing on meadows of snow;

When the blade of youth, hilted with pleasure's gold wreath,
Flashed out of its home like a sword from a sheath,
And advanced o'er the plains. and the hill-tops, to dare
The quick-cutting edge of the frost-tempered air!
How through foaming drifts we careened to and fro,
And tossed the white waves with our ship of the snow,
Which fluttered far back, as we sailed swift along,
A streamer of rich elementary song!

O tall, queenly nights! to eternity's haze
You have followed your short little husbands of days,
But jeweled and braided with youth-freshened strains,
Your memory-ghosts walk the hills and the plains.
Not one of life's glittering subsequent nights,
With feverish pleasures and costly delights,
On treasure-fringed harbors and sail-whitened bays,
Not nights lit with fashion's cold, variable blaze,
Not when the gay opera's beauty-sown song
Plants passion's red flowers in the hearts of the throng;
No nights, dressed in splendor and carried with grace,
Old brave Winter nights, can e'er stand in your place;
Till the long one of death may perhaps bring us nigh
To the star-lighted singing-school held in the sky.

# THE FESTIVAL OF INDUSTRY;

## OR,

# THE COUNTY FAIR.

## I.

THEY brought the best and sleekest of their flocks—
The milkiest cow, the squarest-shouldered ox;
The bull, with mimic thunder in his cry,
And lightning in each eager, wicked eye;

"THE INDIAN CORN-EARS, PRODIGAL OF YIELD."

The sheep that had the heaviest garments worn,
The cock that crowed the loudest in the morn;

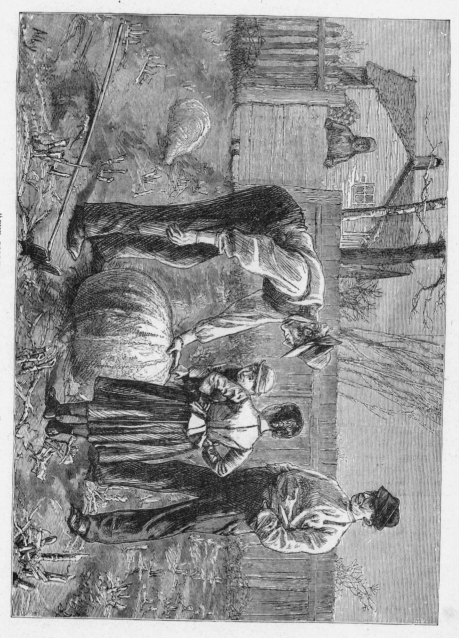

"THE GOLDEN PUMPKIN, NUGGET OF THE FIELD."

The mule, unconscious hypocrite and knave,
The horse, proud high-born Asiatic slave;
The playful calf, with eyes precocious-bright,
The hog—grim quadrupedal appetite;
The Indian corn-ears, prodigal of yield,
The golden pumpkin, nugget of the field;

"THE PEACH—RICH ALTO OF THE ORCHARD'S TUNE."

The merriest-eyed potatoes, nursed in gloom,
Just resurrected from their cradle-tomb;
Rich apples, mellow-cheeked, sufficient all
To 've tempted Eve to fall—to make them fall;
The grapes, whose picking served strong vines to prune,
The peach—rich alto of the orchard's tune;
The very best the farmers' land had grown,
They brought to this menagerie of their own.
But listen! from among the scattered herds
Came to my hearing these equestrian words:

[DIALOGUE OF THE HORSES.]

FIRST HORSE.

We are the pets of men—
The pampered pets of men!
There is naught for us too gentle and good
In the graceful days of our babyhood;
We frisk and caper in childish glee—
Oh, none so pretty and proud as we!
They cheer and cherish us in our play—
Oh, none so smilingly sweet as they!
And when a little our lives have grown,
Each has a table and room his own,
A waiter to fill his bill of fare,
A barber to clean and comb his hair.
        Yes, we are the pets of men!
        The pampered pets of men!
They show us, gayly dressed and proud,
To the eager eyes of the clamorous crowd;
They champion us in the rattling race,
They praise our beauty and cheer our pace;
They keep for us our family trees—
They trumpet our names beyond the seas;
They hang our portraits on their walls,
And paint and garnish and gild our stalls.
        Yes, we are the pets of men—
        The pampered pets of men!


SECOND HORSE.

We are the slaves of men—
The menial slaves of men!
They lash us over the dusty roads,
They bend us down with murderous loads;
They fling vile insults on our track,
And know that we can not answer back;
In winds of Winter, or Summer sun,
The tread of our toil is never done;

And when we are weak, and old, and lame,
And labor-stiffened, and bowed with shame,
And hard of hearing, and blind of eye,
They drive us out in the world to die.
   Yes, we are the slaves of men—
   The slaves of selfish men!
They draft us into their bloody spites,
They spur us, bleeding, into their fights;
They poison our souls with their senseless ire,
And curse us into a storm of fire.
And when to death we are bowed and bent,
And take the ball that for them was meant,
Alone they leave us to groan and bleed,
And dash their spurs in another steed!
   Yes, we are the slaves of men—
   The slaves of brutish men!

## II.

The grim mechanic waved a hardened hand—
Behold! on every side his trophies stand:
The new-made plow, with curving iron beam,
The thresher, with its snowy plume of steam;
The cultivator, stripéd, gay, and proud,
With new ideas and dental wealth endowed;
The windmill, now once more at work for men,
Like some old help discharged and hired again;
The patent churns, whose recommends would seem
To promise butter, almost without cream;
Sewing-machines, of several-woman power,
And destitute of gossip, sweet or sour.
The loud piano raised its voice on high,
And sung the constant chorus, Who will buy?
The patent washer strove to clinch the creed
That cleanliness and laziness agreed;
The reaper, resting idly on its wheel,
Held forth a murderous arm of iron and steel,
And seemed to think 'twas waiting over-long
Before it might begin its rattling song:
9

[SONG OF THE REAPER.]

My grandfather was right little and old,
 And crooked and worn was he;
But his teeth were good, and his heart was bold,
And he swam the waves of a sea of gold,
  But he couldn't keep up with me—me—me—
  Couldn't keep up with me.
Then hie! away to the golden plain!
We will crash and dash through glistening grain,
And gather the wealth of earth and sun,
And the world will eat when our work is done!

My father he was bent and lean,
 But a wide-spread hand had he;
And his fingers they were long and clean,
And he swung his broadsword bright and keen,
  But he never could fight with me—me—me—
  Never could fight with me!
Then hie! away where the sunlight sleeps,
And the wide-floored earth a granary keeps;
We will capture its bushels, one by one,
And the world will eat when our work is done!

The grain-stalk bows his bristling head,
 As I clatter and clash along,
The stubble it bends beneath my tread,
The stacker's yellow tent is spread,
  And the hills throw back my song—my song—
  The hills throw back my song!
Then hie! where the food of nations glows,
And the yellow tide of the harvest flows,
As we dash and crash and glide and run;
And the world will eat when our work is done!


### III.

Edge deftly with me into "Floral Hall,"
Where toil's handwriting, on each crowded wall,

"AS I CLATTER AND CLASH ALONG."

Weighs Industry in balance, o'er and o'er,
And finds the greater part not out-of-door.
The bread loaf, in an unobtrusive place,
Displays its cheerful, honest featured face,
A coin of triumph, from the mintage struck,
Of chemistry, skill, faithfulness, and luck.
What statesman, moulding laws, can understand
The far-eyed cunning of a housewife's hand?
What queen her subjects with more anxious eyes
Can watch, than she her "emptyings," as they rise?
What conquest gives what warrior more delight
Than she has, when her baking comes out right?
(Ah me! we oft know not, till over-late,
What things are truly small, and what are great!
'Tis sometimes hard to tell, in God's vast sky,
What's actually low, and what is high!)
Here rests, not over-free from pain and ache,
Bread's proud, rich, city-nurtured cousin, Cake:
Gay-plumaged as his sisters are, the pies—
Food chiefly for the palate and the eyes.
These canned fruits, like the four-and-twenty birds
Imprisoned in the nursery ballad's words,
Will be expected, when at last released,
To sing sweet taste-songs for some Winter feast.
Proudly displayed, rich trophies there are found
Of the fierce needle's thread-strewn battle-ground:
This is a bed-quilt—its credentials show—
Stitched by a grandame, centuries ago;
That is embroidery, made this very year,
By some unteened miss, who is lurking near.
The picture family is abroad to-day,
Dressed up in every gaze-enticing way:
Here an oil-painting pleads for truthful art,
Wrought by some local genius with his heart;
He sighs to see his soul misunderstood,
And hear them call the picture "pr'tty good."
Work on, poor boy, with courage that endures:
Stars have burst forth from blacker clouds than yours.

Feel with your own heart—think with your own mind,
And make the canvas speak the thoughts they find!
The eyes may not be very far away
That will, on some glad, unexpected day,
Bring other eyes within your strange control,
And lift your name along-side of your soul.
This is the town photographer's display;
Who shows his showiest patrons here to-day.
He places in his pillory of frames
The faces of the town's most talked-of names:
The mayor, with his eyebrows stiffly arched,
And collar unconditionally starched,
Shows, through this careful chemical design,
His last majority, in every line.
His wife hangs in an advantageous place,
With new-discovered beauties in her face,
From the sun-artist's thrifty, cunning trade:
Photography, you are a flatt'ring jade!
Some of their subjects dangling here are found—
A settlement of faces clusters round—
A kind of kingdom, as it were, in sport:
The mayor holding photographic court.
Each one in half-fictitious splendor 's dressed,
And each is doing his pictorial best.
The artist, grinning down a look of gall,
Worked for these baby-pictures most of all;
Dear, dear! how low he had to bow and scrape,
To keep his infant popinjays in shape,
And hold the sinless villain's glance in check,
To save his shadow enterprise from wreck!
To keep this little wandering Arab-eye
He made himself a miscellaneous guy;
He was this petty tyrant's vassal true,
His portrait-painter, and court-jester, too;
And, that a first-class picture might be done,
Made himself into a ridiculous one;
Said "Hooty-tooty," and that sort of thing,
And made the rattle-box insanely sing.

"THAN SHE HAS, WHEN HER BAKING COMES OUT RIGHT?"

But, passing from these posy-sprinkled bowers
(For children's features are the facial flowers),
Come with me, where white hands have thickly strown
The horticultural house-pets they have grown.
What are but weeds beneath a southern sky,
Are here, as house-plants, rated precious-high;
As villains go to uncongenial climes,
But, being less known, have better social times.
(So our old Mullein, here of deference scant,
Struts round in England as " The Velvet Plant;"
And "Cactus"—Thistle when in south-land met—
Is here a prickly flower, to keep and pet.)
But woman's wand-like nature can, indeed,
Make beauty spring from e'en a common weed;
How much more, when, around some flower-gem rare
She throws the setting of her tender care!
Sweet window-gardeners! with dainty arts
Tracing the floral language of your hearts,
Making The Home, with these gay-liveried slaves,
A bloom-fed island 'mid the winter-waves;
In which the frost-bit caller can commune
With bright hours stolen from some day in June.
'Tis your sweet, cultured taste that bids us call
This niche of labor's temple " Floral Hall."


## IV.

The people stood about on every side,
And keenly these familiar wonders eyed,
Each minute seeking some new ocular prize;
But, as they gazed about, their greedy eyes
On nothing queerer than mankind could fall,
And so they watched each other most of all.
There was the thrifty farmer: quickly he
Had seen about all that he wished to see,
And knew, while up and down condemned to roam,
How much more he should feel at home, at home.
The farmer's wife, with smiles of rural grace
O'erflowing from her soul into her face,

Screamed loud as each acquaintance hove in view,
And gave the cordial cry, "How *dew* you dew?"
The farmer's boy bore vigor in his tread,
And in his hands a block of gingerbread;
The farmer's girl was, somewhat prone to flirt,
Watched by her mother, lest she come to hurt;
Whose words had full as much effect as when,
Around some pond, an anxious-eyed old hen
To draw away her gosling-children strives,
And take them from their life, to save their lives.
The doctors, lawyers, merchants, and that kind,
Looked round, their old-time customers to find,
Or shun—and smiling 'mid the verbal din,
Dilated on *their* country origin.
A writer for the Agricultural Press,
Who farmed (on foolscap) with complete success,
Who raised great crops of produce in a wink,
And tilled large farms with paper, pen, and ink—
Who, sitting in-door, at a regular price,
Gave large amounts of good out-door advice,
And, as his contribution to the Fair,
Had brought himself and an oration there—
Arose, in somewhat over-conscious strength,
And gave his views at any amount of length.
As when the sun at morning upward crowds
His kingly path through thickly gathered clouds,
Sometimes, behold! these vapor-birds have flown,
Driven by his rays, and left him there alone,
So from this luminary, fancy-fired,
The saddened audience gradually retired;
Though still stayed where they were when he began,
Three children, and a very deaf old man.
And even these showed signs of weakening,
When the sad poet rose, and with a fling
Of paper that a ragman might rejoice,
Remarked, in timidly defiant voice:
"Spirits of earth-dead agriculturists!
If the ghost ear to rhythmic nonsense lists

(And if I have a hearing, that must be,
For I'm not jostled by mortality)—
Spirits, if you should deem attention due
To one who soon must starve his way to you
(A process that this rich world, by-the-way,
Is aiding quietly, from day to day,
Seeming to think the poet's proper place
Is 'mongst his own—ahem!—angelic race),
Oh list to me, said spirits, here declare
My contribution to the County Fair
To be a drop of rhythm from off my pen,
Which I denominate

## THE LABORING MEN.

Who are the laboring men?
We are the laboring men:
We, the muscle of tribes and lands,
With sun-trod faces and horn-gloved hands;
With well patched garments, stained and coarse—
With untrained voices, heavy and hoarse;
Who brave the death of the noontide heats—
Who mow the meadows and pave the streets;
Who push the plow by the smooth faced sod,
Or climb the crags with a well filled hod.
Yes—we are the laboring men—
The genuine laboring men!
And each, somewhere in the stormy sky,
Has a sweet love-star, be it low or high;
For pride have we to do and dare,
And a heart have we—to cherish and care;
And power have we: for lose our brawn,
And where were your flourishing cities gone?
Or bind our hands or fetter our feet,
And what would the gaunt world find to eat?
Ay, where were your gentry then?
For we are the laboring men!

Who are the laboring men?
We are the laboring men:
We who stand in the ranks of trade,
And count the tallies that toil has made;
Who guard the coffers of wealth untold,
And ford the streams of glistening gold;
Who send the train in its breathless trips,
And rear the buildings, and sail the ships;
And though our coats be a trifle fine,
And though our diamonds flash and shine,
   Yet we are the laboring men—
   The genuine laboring men!
We bolt the gates of the angry seas;
We keep the nation's granary keys;
The routes of trade we have built and planned
Are veins of life to a hungry land.
And power have we in our peaceful strife,
For a nation's trade is a nation's life;
And take the sails of our commerce in,
Where were your "artisans' pails of tin?"
   Ay, where were your "laborers" then?
   For we are the laboring men!

Who are the laboring men?
We are the laboring men:
We of the iron and water-way,
Whom fire and steam, and tide obey;
Who stab the sea with a prow of oak—
Who blot the sky with a cloud of smoke;
Who bend the breezes unto our wills,
And feed the looms and hurry the mills;
Who oft have the lives of a thousand known,
In the hissing valves that hold our own!
   Yes, we are the laboring men—
   The genuine laboring men!
And though a coat may a button lack,
And though a face be sooty and black,
And though the words be heavy of flow,
And new-called thoughts come tardy and slow,

And though rough words in a speech may blend,
A heart's a heart, and a friend's a friend!
And power have we: but for our skill,
The wave would drown, and the sea would kill;
   And where were your gentry then?
   Ay, we are the laboring men!

   Who are the laboring men?
   We are the laboring men:
We of the mental toil and strain,
Who stall the body and lash the brain;
Who wield our pen when the world's asleep,
And plead with mortals to laugh or weep;
Who bind the wound and plead the cause,
Who preach the sermons and make the laws,
Who man the stage for the listening throng,
And fight the devils of Shame and Wrong.
   Yes, we are the laboring men—
   The genuine laboring men!
And though our hands be small and white,
And though our flesh be tender and light,
And though our muscle be soft and low,
Our red-blood-sluices are swift of flow!
We've power to kindle Passion's fire
With the flame of rage and fell desire;
Or quell, with soothing words and arts,
To throbs of grief, the leaping hearts.
   And who shall question, then,
   That we are the laboring men?

   Who are NOT the laboring men?
   They're not the laboring men:
They who creep in dens and lanes,
To rob their betters of honest gains;
The rich that stoop to devour the poor;
The tramps that beg from door to door;
The rogues who love a darkened sky,
And steal and rob, and cheat and lie;

The loafing wights and senseless bloats
Who drain their pockets to wet their throats!
        They're not the laboring men—
        The genuine laboring men!
And all true hearts that the price would give
For honest joy and a right to live,
And every soul to truth alive,
Willing to thrive and let others thrive,
Should rise with a true and steady hand.
And mark these foes with a villain-brand;
And shame them into the ranks of toil,
Or crush them under their kindred soil,
        Away from the laboring men—
        The genuine laboring men!


## V.

Before the reading of this rhyme had ceased,
A crowd near by, that gradually increased,
Had gathered round a tramp, old, bent, and gray,
Who somehow through the gates had made his way,
For human pity rather than for pelf:
This clanless gypsy, wandering by himself.
No face and brow more wrinkles could have worn;
His clothes were most spectacularly torn;
But something in his general effect
Drew from the throng a rough, unkempt respect;
For crushed old age, in heart-enlightened lands,
Carries a pathos with it that commands.
He had been talking to the one most near:
Those standing by were not averse to hear,
And soon about him formed a massive ring;
His audience swelled like valley-streams in spring.
Crowds gather crowds by wondrous swift degrees;
One comes to see what 'tis another sees.
For curiosity has ever shown
A greedy-grasping avarice of its own,
And few there are in this world, high or low,
Who do not like to know what others know.

He, with no oratorical display,
Spoke to the farmers in their own rough way,
And they looked at him as some prophet cast
Out of the dusty cobwebs of the past,
With nineteenth century rags about him hung,
And current lack of grammar on his tongue.
He *was* a prophet; for he clear could see
The past—dead father of what is to be;
He who *what has been* faithfully can tell,
May prophesy the future pretty well.
With half-defiant and half-modest air,
His sad eyes flashing, and his silver hair
Tinged by the sun's last rays of autumn-gold—
This is the story that the old man told:

### [THE TRAMP'S STORY.]

If experience has gold in it (as discerning folks agree)
Then there's quite a little fortune stowed away somewhere in me,
And I deal it out regardless of a regular stated price,
In rough-done-up prize packages of common-sense advice;
The people they can take it, or run round it, as they please;
But the best thing they'll find in it is some words like unto these:

*Worm or beetle—drought or tempest—on a farmer's land may fall;
But for first-class ruination, trust a mortgage 'gainst them all.*

On my weddin'-day my father touched me kindly on the arm,
And handed me the papers for an eighty acre farm,
With the stock an' tools an' buildin's for an independent start;
Saying, "Here's a wedding present from my muscle and my heart;
And, except the admonitions you have taken from my tongue,
And the reasonable lickin's that you had when you was young,
And your food and clothes and schoolin' (not so much as I could wish,
For I had a number eatin' from a some'at scanty dish),
And the honest love you captured when you first sat on my knee.
This is all I have to give you—so expect no more from me."

People 'd said I couldn't marry the sweet girl I tried to court,
Till we smilingly submitted a minority report;

Then they laid their theories over, with a quickness queer to see
And said they knew we'd marry, but we never could agree;
But we did not frame and hang up all the neighbors had to say,
But ran our little heaven in our own peculiar way;
We started off quite jolly, wondrous full of health and cheer,
And a general understanding that the road was pretty clear.

So we lived and toiled and prospered; and the little family party
That came on from heaven to visit us were bright, and hale, and hearty;
And to-day we might ha' been there, had I only just have known
How to lay my road down solid, and let well enough alone.
But I soon commenced a-kicking in the 'traces, I confess;
There was too much land that joined me that I didn't yet possess.
When once he gets land-hungry, strange how ravenous one can be!
'Twasn't long before I wanted all the ground that I could see.
So I bought another eighty (not foreboding any harm),
And for that and some down-money put a mortgage on my farm.
Then I bought another forty—hired some cash to fix up new—
And to buy a covered carriage, and of course the mortgage grew.
Now my wife was square against this, 'tis but right that you should
        know
(Though I'm very far from saying that I think it's *always* so);
But she went in hearty with me, working hard from day to day,
For we knew that life was business, now we had that debt to pay.

We worked through spring and winter—through summer and through
        fall—
But that mortgage worked the hardest and the steadiest of us all;
It worked on nights and Sundays—it worked each holiday—
It settled down among us, and it never went away.
Whatever we kept from it seemed a'most as bad as theft;
It watched us every minute, and it ruled us right and left.
The rust and blight were with us sometimes, and sometimes not;
The dark-browed, scowling mortgage was forever on the spot.
The weevil and the cut-worm, they went as well as came;
The mortgage staid forever, eating hearty all the same.
It nailed up every window—stood guard at every door—
And happiness and sunshine made their home with us no more.

"THE DOGS HOWL CURSES AT ME, AND HUNT ME DOWN THE ROAD."

Till with failing crops and sickness we got stalled upon the grade,
And there came a dark day on us when the interest wasn't paid;
And there came a sharp foreclosure, and I kind o' lost my hold,
And grew weary and discouraged, and the farm was cheaply sold.
The children left and scattered when they hardly yet were grown;
My wife she pined an' perished, an' I found myself alone.
What she died of was "a mystery," an' the doctors never knew;
But *I* knew she died of *mortgage*—just as well 's I wanted to.
If to trace a hidden sorrow were within the doctors' art,
They'd ha' found a mortgage lying on that woman's broken heart.

Two different kinds of people the devil most assails:
One is the man who conquers—the other he who fails.
But still I think the last kind are soonest to give up,
And to hide their sorry faces behind the shameful cup;
Like some old king or other, whose name I've somehow lost,
They straightway tear their eyes out, just when they need 'em most.
When once I had discovered that the debt I could not pay,
I tried to liquidate it in a rather common way:
I used to meet in private a fellow-financier,
And we would drink ourselves worth ten thousand dollars clear;
As easy a way to prosper as ever has been found;
But one's a heap sight poorer when he gets back to the ground.

Of course I ought to ha' braced up, an' worked on all the same;
I ain't a-tryin' to shirk out, or cover up from blame;
But still I think men often, it safely may be said,
Are *driven* to temptations in place of being led;
And if that tyrant mortgage hadn't cracked its whip at me,
I shouldn't have constituted the ruin that you see.
For though I've never stolen or defaulted, please to know,
Yet, socially considered, I am pretty middlin' low.

I am helpless an' forsaken—I am childless an' alone;
I haven't a single dollar that it's fair to call my own;
My old age knows no comfort, my heart is scant o' cheer,
The children they run from me as soon as I come near.
The women shrink and tremble—their alms are fear-bestowed—
The dogs howl curses at me, and hunt me down the road.

My home is where night finds me; my friends are few and cold;
Oh, little is there in this world for one who's poor and old!
But I'm wealthy in experience, all put up in good advice,
To take or not to take it—with no difference in the price;
You may have it, an' thrive on it, or run round it, as you please,
But I generally give it wrapped in some such words as these:

*Worm or beetle—drought or tempest—on a farmer's land may fall;*
*But for first-class ruination, trust a mortgage 'gainst them all.*

# THE FESTIVAL OF INJUSTICE;

OR,

## THE LAWSUIT.

THERE was a lawsuit in our town:
Two honest farmers, White and Brown,
Who'd been near neighbors all their lives,
Had from the same home lured their wives,
Had interchanged celestial views,
On Sundays, from adjoining pews,
Subjecting thus, in the same church,
Their neighbors' sins to weekly search;
Had shared each golden Christmas chime,
And "changed works" every harvest time;
Had felt a partnership, half hid,
In everything they said and did;
Had always, on town-meeting day,
Talked, yelled, and voted both one way;
Who each, whate'er he wished to do,
Had all the influence of the two
(And two united, as men run,
Are more than twice as strong as one);
Whose children, through youth's sun and shade,
Had with each other fought and played—
These men fell out, one raw March day,
In something like the following way:

White had a sheep he boasted o'er:
Value two dollars—maybe more.
Brown did a brindle dog possess;
Value, two cents, or maybe less.

10*

The sheep, one night, was killed by stealth;
The dog retained his usual health.
White felt the separation-shock
As if the sheep had been a flock;
And reaped a crop of mental blues
(We always value what we lose).
Brown's heart the theory could not hear.
Which White propounded to his ear,
That his dog's life should make amends
(No cur so mean but has his friends).
White vowed, in words profanely deep,
That Brown's canine had killed his sheep
(Which accusation was o'er-true;
The dog himself well knew it, too).
Brown, unconvinced and anger-eyed,
Insisted that his neighbor lied.
White skirmished round, by day and night,
In hopes to shoot the dog at sight;
Brown kenneled him beneath his bed,
And sent bad language out instead.
Suit for the sheep was brought by White;
Brown fought him back with all his might.
Thus are the reasons jotted down,
Why we'd a lawsuit in our town.

White's lawyer was, when fairly weighed,
The meanest of that tempted trade;
With all the vices of his clan,
And not a virtue known to man.
In almost every calling, he
Had shown how little, men can be;
Had demonstrated, teaching schools,
That small men can be monstrous fools,
And by strong pupils, once or more,
Was taught the object of the door;
Had preached awhile, at his own call,
With hearers few, or none at all
(For souls to cling are seldom prone
Round men who have none of their own);

"WHITE VOWED, IN WORDS PROFANELY DEEP,
THAT BROWN'S CANINE HAD KILLED HIS SHEEP."

At farming once had tried his hand,
But laziness grows poor on land.
He had, for half a month or more,
Been salesman in a country store,
Where, though his talents he ne'er hid,
Some of the cash somebody did;
And he, before his sphere enlarged,
By his employer was discharged.
Then his frouzed head and lantern-jaw
Had fin'lly drifted toward the law
(Not *to* it—candor must admit—
But only just in sight of it);
And so he took a dead-head trip,
On pettifoggery's pirate ship,
Coming at last, it may be said,
To be its brazen figure-head.
This wolf became, at one fell leap,
Attorney for White's missing sheep.
Brown's lawyer equal praise would bear;
Ah me! they were a pretty pair!

Such villains cast no shade of blame
On any honest lawyer's name;
There are those do not hew their life
Into the kindling-wood of strife,
To fire men's hearts and homes in turn,
That they may rob them as they burn;
Who only take such causes as
The eternal Right already has;
Who, when a client comes along
Upon the fragile stilts of wrong,
And strives to make law help him bear
His weight through Error's putrid air,
Show him the sin on which he's bent,
Induce him, maybe, to repent,
And send him home, with altered plan,
A wiser and not poorer man.
Such, with strong heart, and head, and hand,
Are benefactors to the land;

It is not to the craft's disgrace
That there were none such in this case.

Scarce did the rage-envenomed din
Have leisure fairly to begin,
Through the thick crowd an old man strode,
Making himself a ragged road;
With gestures lower than his looks,
Upset a pile of huge law-books,
Inked a half-quire of legal cap,
Also Brown's lawyer's left-hand lap;
Ignoring, with a scorn profound,
The judge and jury clustering round,
He climbed his greatest tiptoe-height,
And made this speech to Brown and White:

So you're at it, sure enough—
Side-hold, square-hold, kick and cuff—
Any way to down each other, if it's only brought about;
With two rogues in your employ,
For to hollo out " S't boy !"
An' to superintend your pockets, an' pick up what rattles out.

An' your folks, too, it appears,
Have been gettin' by the ears,
All prepared to hate each other, for forever an' a day;
The devil gives a shout
When a family falls out;
But what is that to you 'uns, if you only have your way?

An' your friends an' neighbors, too,
Have been wranglin' over you;
Your example has been followed, as to brother fightin' brother;
There is more bad blood round here
Than 'll drain off in a year;
But what is that to you 'uns, if you only bleed each other?

Can our church such things endure?
You're agoin' to bu'st it, sure!

An' the hosts of sin are ready to begin their triumph-revel;
    But what would you 'uns give
    To save all the souls that live,
So you just can clinch together, an' go rolling toward the devil?

    And the Lord that o'er us reigns:
    He has taken extra pains
For to put you two in harness, so's to pull together square;
    'Stead o' which you kick an' bite,
    With a reg'lar ten-mule spite;
Do you think that, strictly speaking, you're a-treatin' on Him fair?

    O you law-bamboozled fools!
    You old self-ground devil's-tools!
Do you know you're sowin' ruin out o' hell's half-acre lot?
    Do you know when smart men fight
    They Calamity invite,
Who comes round an' stays forever, till he eats up all they've got?

    O you poor cat's-paws of spite!
    Ain't there 'nough things for to fight—
Ain't there rust an' blight an' tempest—ain't there misery sore an' deep—
    Ain't there ignorance an' wrong,
    An' what woes to them belong,
But that you must fight each other 'bout a brindle dog and sheep?

    Why, man is just one race,
    In a very ticklish place,
With a thousand forces fightin' for to lay him on the shelf;
    Don't it strike you, foolish men,
    As a losin' business, then,
When he tears down his defenses, an' goes fightin' of himself?

    An' these lawyers round here gawkin'—
    Who has tried to stop my talkin'—
If they come it once too often, I—I vow I'll smash 'em both;
    What d'ye s'pose they care for *you*,
    Or for what *they* say or do?
For they don't pay no expenses, an' they ain't put under oath.

Shake han's now, an' be friends,
An' say, Here the matter ends,
An' divide the costs between you—what has so far been incurred;
It'll make this world less sad—
It'll make all heaven glad!
"Peace on earth," is just as good news as the angels ever heard.


Here the judge spoke, with angry air:
"We have no jurisdiction there;
It's more than all our work is worth,
To keep things steady here on earth;
We can't pretend, best we can do,
To litigate for angels too.
I hereby fine you, for this sport,
Ten dollars, for contempt of court,
And you will in the jail be laid,
Until the little sum is paid.
Remove this person from the place,
And let us go on with the case."


With look most cheerful and polite,
The old man turned to Brown and White,
Saying, "For your good I made this speech:
Pray lend me now, five dollars each.
I've been a-throwin' you advice
You couldn't ha' bought at any price.
If you will give my words an ear,
They're worth ten thousan' dollars clear."


His eloquence had no avail;
They took the old man off to jail.
The suit went on—please don't forget—
And, I believe, isn't finished yet.

# THE FESTIVAL OF DIS-REASON;

## OR,

## THE DEBATE.

THEY came in sleighs and cutters down the snow-paved country
  road—
No farm-house in the district but sent something of "a load,"
No home so high or humble, but threw in its mental mite
Toward an equitable judgment on the issue of the night;
For the question to be settled was an elemental one:
Namely, whether fire or water had the greater damage done.

O Peace! thy famous mantle is a lovely thing to view,
But what unimportant matters can suffice to tear it through!
Now a three-month had this "district" been by thee as much inspired,
As a first-class summer evening, when the sun has just retired;
Till some indiscreet debater fired the battle's signal gun,
Asking whether fire or water had the greater damage done.

As when the housewife, whisking through her culinary toil,
Bathes the inside of a kettle, it will foam and seethe and boil,
As when a brawny blacksmith, his hot iron all agleam,
Stabs the unsuspecting water, it will hiss and yell and scream,
So the most pronounced convulsions it had ever known as yet,
Made life lively in this neighborhood when fire and water met.

Not when the choir, one Sunday, chirped a secular-sounding song;
Not when the pastor married diametrically wrong;
Not when the new school-master, with a sweet and cheerful smile,
Flogged three champion school-house bullies in improved athletic style;

Had there been so fierce excitement.—Naught more bitter words can
    make,
Than discussion where the parties haven't any thing at stake.

O War! thy grim material pauses not at guns and swords:
There are campaigns of opinion—there are carnages of words!
Now that neighborhood, so peaceful till this unexpected day,
Formed itself, as if by magic, in belligerent array,
Full of empty emulation, and disinterested ire;
About half denouncing water—the remainder fighting fire.

There were deadly feuds engendered, in that clash of word and will,
That have crept through generations, and are living even still;
There were families imbittered—sacred friendships rent in twain—
In that well-nigh useless contest of the heart and of the brain.
For the fight on this occasion had grown bitter and intense,
In proportion as the issue was of little consequence.

Old Squire Taylor took his children out of school, without delay,
When the teacher taught Volcanoes in an underhanded way;
Deacon Stebbins, it was whispered, gave his son a whipping rare,
Just for drawing on the Deluge in his verse at morning prayer;
And the good but shrewd old preacher—half in love and half in fear—
Scarcely mentioned fire or water in his sermons for a year.

There were fisticuffs and lawsuits bred among the brawny men—
Women who ne'er borrowed sugar at each other's house again;
And the children called their playmates, when they fell out, in their
    games,
"Water-fowl," and "Papa's fire-bug," and such-like endearing names;
While a keen demand existed 'mongst the people, great and small,
For the evening when this question should be settled once for all.

They came in sleds and cutters down the snow-paved country roads;
They swarmed like bees in anger, from the depths of their abodes;
They urged their bell-fringed coursers; they hurried, with one will,
To the little old red school-house at the summit of the hill.
For 'twas there that the discussion was appointed to take place,
And the fiercest of debaters meet each other face to face.

"NO PRESTIGE WAS RESPECTED, IN THE STORM OF RAGE THAT ROSE."

O little old red school-house! your prosperous days are flown!
You are a sad old school-house, decrepit and alone.
Within your grimly ruins, now half crumbled to the ground,
The wind repeats its lessons, in a listless, droning sound;
The snow-flakes leap your windows, and cluster on your floor,
Or, like belated youngsters, creep slyly through the door;

No more incipient maidens softly to your portals come,
With pantalettes of nankeen, and surreptitious gum;
No more the idle urchin, wrapped in secret hardihood,
Daily strives to make you useful in the line of kindling-wood;
No more the youthful chalk-fiend traces incoherent scrawls,
And startling hieroglyphics, on your dim and dingy walls;

Your painted rival perches on the yonder neighboring hill;
The restless feet that sought you are lying very still.
The flowers of many summers upon their graves have grown;
You are a sad old school-house, decrepit and alone.
But you have had your triumphs; and, if accounts be right,
You were not over-lonely on that famous winter night!

Oh, what a crowd had gathered, and how wide awake they were,
To see this mighty struggle of the elements occur!
The buds and blooms of beauty of that region had turned out,
Also all the brain and muscle of the country round about;
For, as some one gravely mentioned—'twas an interesting time—
A trial whose attorneys gloried in their clients' crime.

There was Corporal Joseph Bellamy, a veteran fierce and gray,
Whose left leg took a furlough on the field of Monterey,
And who whispered, "How'd the Waterites get away, he'd like to know,
With the fire that burned the powder in our war with Mexico?"
There was Captain Abel Stockwell, who the raging main had ploughed,
And had some old claim of wreckage which he wished to get allowed;

There was Andrew Clark, a bully, who remarked, he couldn't debate,
But could lick the biggest waterin'-trough that spouted in the State;
There was pretty Jessie Miller, with her blushing face half hid,
Who didn't say much on the question—just because her lover did;

11

There was " Uncle Sammy," smiling gay and happy—nothing loth
To dispute with either faction, or, if necessary, both;

There was dear old Sister Dibble, amiable and pleasant-eyed,
Who agreed with all she talked to, and no matter on which side;
There was Uncle James K. Hopkins, who espoused one cause to-day,
And to-morrow morning early, always thought the other way;
There was Township Treasurer Hawley, who a theory could frame,
That The Law of Compensation made them both destroy the same;

There was Road Commissioner Reynolds, who, as president, would state
The true meaning of the question they had come there to debate;
But was checked by Uncle Sammy, with his back firm 'gainst the wall,
Who declared, as if astonished, that that wasn't it at all!
So an hour they wrangled, trying to discover, beyond doubt,
What it was that all the people had been quarreling about.

As well might be imagined, 'twas a trifle ludicrous
To hear this crowd discussing as to what they should discuss;
Until the conversation reached the pure assertive stage,
The pattering of word-drops turned to thunder-peals of rage,
And young Napoleon Peaslee, with his black eyes opened wide,
Shook his fist at several others, and informed them that they lied.

When this argument was stated ('tis a not uncommon one),
Andrew Clark bobbed up his body, like the rammer of a gun
When the load at last is driven, and remarked, with aspect hot,
That into his department the discussion now had got;
Then, striding o'er three benches, to the speaker he drew nigh,
And advanced a heavy argument at Napoleon's nearest eye.

As when the thrifty farmer his cold yard with fodder strews,
Two sturdy youthful bullocks will develop different views,
And join belligerent issue—then their rage infects the herd,
Till the peacefulest old mulley feels her blood with battle stirred,
So this meeting joined in conflict; and affairs assumed a shape
As if sin's unpleasant future had effected an escape.

No prestige was respected, in the storm of rage that rose;
The deacon shook ten knuckles underneath the elder's nose;

The squire upset the sheriff, with undignified display,
When the latter "Peace" demanded, in a very warlike way;
And even Sister Dibble her fat fist to shake began,
And vowed to goodness gracious that she wished she was a man!

E'en the stove—a shattered veteran, which for many years had stood
On two legs, and two frail crutches made of bricks and blocks of wood,
And, like some worthy people who are nothing if not plumb,
Had no single earthly merit save its equilibrium,
Lost even that; and, falling 'mid this clash of frantic souls,
Smashed, and emptied out a bushel of the liveliest kind of coals.

As when the juvenile shepherd scares his flock of timid sheep
Through the narrows of a fence-gap, they will rush and plunge and
        leap,
So the bravest, and the strongest, and the fiercest that were there,
Loitered not upon their journey to the free and open air;
Which, flying from their presence, rushed into the open door,
And scattered coals and fire-brands all about the school-house floor.

"It's a-burnin' up the buildin'!" was the universal shout:
"We'll be taxed to build another, if we do not put it out!"
The debaters, each forgetting his rhetoric ends and aims,
Rushed in with snow and water, to subdue the rising flames;
And 'twas even hard to tell there, when the victory was won,
Whether fire or whether water had the greater damage done.

They drove their sleighs and cutters homeward o'er the snowy road;
Their clothes were wet and freezing—their hearts with anger glowed:
E'en those agreeing differed; cutting up the question, they
Disagreed on its divisions, and disputed by the way.
And only one was happy who to this affair had come;
And he was under-witted, and was also deaf and dumb.

O thinkers and debaters! be moderate and more slow;
You can't make true opinions—they have to seed and grow.
Be generous in your conflicts; look very sharp to see
What points you can discover whereon you may agree;
Remember, mere assertion to mere brutishness comes nigh,
And the shallowest of arguments is the poisoned words, "You lie!"

# THE FESTIVAL OF REUNION;

OR,

## THE GOLDEN WEDDING.

WAKE up, wife!—the black cloak of Night begins to fade,
And far in the east The Morning his kitchen fire has made;
And he is heating red-hot his stove of iron-gray,
And stars are winking and blinking before the light o' day.

Mind you what I was doin', just fifty years agone?—
Brushing my Sunday raiment an' puttin' my best looks on;
Clothin' myself in courage, so none my fright would see;
An' my coward heart within, the while, was pounding to get free!

Ten mile wood an' bramble, and three mile field an' dew,
In the cold smile of morning, I walked, to marry you;
No horse had I but my wishes—no pilot but a star;
But my boyish heart it fancied it heard you from afar!

So through the woods I hurried, an' through the grass an' dew,
An' little I thought o' tiring, the whole of my journey through;
Things ne'er before nor after do so a man rejoice,
As on the day he marries the woman of his choice!

And then our country wedding—brimful o' grief an' glee,
With every one a-pettin' an' jokin' you an' me;
The good cheer went and came, wife, as it sometimes has done
When clouds have chased each other across the Summer sun.

There was your good old father, dressed up in weddin' shape,
With all the homespun finery that he could rake an' scrape;

"AND THE PARSON'S VIRGIN DAUGHTER, PLAIN AND SEVERELY PURE,
WHO HOPED WE SHOULD BE HAPPY, BUT WASN'T EXACTLY SURE."

And your dear-hearted mother, the sunlight of whose smile
Shone through the showers of tear-drops that stormed her face the
      while;

Also your sisters an' brothers, who hardly seemed to know
How they could scare up courage to let their sister go;
An' cousins an' school-house comrades, dressed up in meetin' trim,
With one of them a-sulkin' because it wasn't him;

An' there was the good old parson, his neck all dressed in white,
A bunch o' texts in his left eye, a hymn-book in his right;
And the parson's virgin daughter, plain an' severely pure,
Who hoped we should be happy, but wasn't exactly sure;

And there was the victuals, seasoned with kind regards an' love,
And holly-wreaths with breastpins of rubies, up above;
An' there was my heart a-wonderin' as how such things could be,
And there was the world before us, and there was you and me.

Wake up, wife! that gold bird, the Sun, has come in sight,
And on a tree-top perches to take his daily flight!
He is not old and feeble; an' he will sail away,
As he has done so often since fifty years to-day.

You know there's company coming—our daughters an' our sons:
There's John, and James, and Lucy, an' all their little ones;
And Jennie, she will be here, who in her grave doth lie
(Provided company ever can come from out the sky);

And Sam—I am not certain as he will come, or not;
They say he is a black sheep—the wildest of the lot.
Before a son's dishonor, a father's love stands dumb;
But still, somehow or other, I hope that Sam will come!

The tree bends down its branches to its children from above—
The son is lord of the father, and rules him with his love;
And he will e'er be longed for, though far they be apart,
For the drop of blood he carries, that came from the father's heart.

Wake you, wife! the loud sun has roused the sweet Daylight,
And she has dressed herself up in red and yellow and white;
She has dressed herself for us, wife—for our weddin'-day once more—
And my soul to-day is younger than ever it was before!

# THE FESTIVAL OF MEMORY;

OR,

## CONVERSE WITH THE SLAIN.

[Read at the National Cemetery on the Custis Farm, Arlington Heights, Va., Decoration Day, 1877.]

HERE where the Nation's domes salute our eye,
And lift their fingers up to freedom's sky,
Here where, by green-flagged hill and flowery glade,
Camps evermore the Nation's dead brigade,
And, though our stars upon the day are tossed,
White, gleaming head-stones tell of what they cost,
And Triumph's guns are decked with Sorrow's strain,
Let us hold converse with the Nation's slain.

### I.

Strong men fast asleep,
    With coverlets wrought of clay,
Do soft dreams o'er you creep,
    Of friends who are here to-day?
Do you know, O men low lying
    In the hard and chilly bed,
That we, the slowly dying,
    Are giving a day to the dead?
Do you know that sighs for your deaths
    Across our heart-strings play,
E'en from the last faint breaths
    Of the sweet-lipped mouth of May?
When you fell, at Duty's call,
    Your fame it glittered high,

As leaves of the sombre Fall
    Grow brighter though they die.
Men of the silent bands,
    Men of the half-told days,
Lift up your spectre hands,
    And take our heart-bouquets.

[ RESPONSE. ]

Our heads droop on the world's broad breast;
Our work is done, and we have gone to rest.
These footsteps, lingering round our bed,
The sun that shines, the storm that sweeps o'erhead,
The summer hour, when naught sounds nigh
Save the low, drowsy humming of the fly,
Or the wind's moan when day is done,
All feed our sleep, and all to us are one.

When morning sows the sky with gold,
To blossom forth at noon a million-fold,
When, shaded from the setting sun,
The weary father clasps his little one,
While she whose chastened love ne'er dies
Leans on them with her patient mother-eyes,
When the brown frame of even-time
Is pictured deep with song and laughter's chime;

Of all these sweet and pure and blest,
Not one avails to call us from our rest.
Fought we for wealth?  We own, to-day,
Death's tattered robes, and six good feet of clay.
For noisy Fame's bright coronets?
The world applauds us, but it soon forgets.
And yet, on royal robes we fall:
We fought for Love—and Love is king of all.

.

## II.

Women, whose rich graves deck
    The work of Strife's red spade,

"LET US HOLD CONVERSE WITH THE NATION'S SLAIN."

Shining wrecks of the wreck
    This tempest of war has made,
You whose sweet pure love
    Round every suffering twined,
Whose hearts, like the sky above,
    Bent o'er all human kind,
Who walked through hospital streets,
    'Twixt white abodes of pain,
Counting the last heart-beats
    Of men who were slowly slain;
Whose thrilling voices ever
    Such words of comfort bore,
That many a poor boy never
    Such music had heard before;
Whose deeds were so sweet and gracious,
    Wherever your light feet trod,
That every step seemed precious,
    As if it were that of God;
Whose eyes so divinely beamed,
    Whose touch was so tender and true,
That the dying soldier dreamed
    Of the purest love he knew;
O martyrs of more than duty!
    Sweet-hearted woman-braves!
Did you think, in this day's sad beauty,
    That we could forget your graves?
Could you think, of these yearning hours,
    None from your memory grew?
That we brought a garden of flowers,
    And never a blossom for you?
Great is the brave commander,
    With foemen round him slain,
But greater far, and grander,
    Is she who can soothe a pain.
Not till selfish blindness
    Has clouded every eye,
Not till mercy and kindness
    Have flown back to the sky,

Not till a heart that is human
　　Within this world beats not,
Shall the kind deeds of a woman
　　Be ever by man forgot.
Heaven's best evangels,
　　Artists of mercy's arts,
Earth-types of the angels,
　　Take these flowers from our hearts.

[ RESPONSE. ]

Sound and deep our bodies sleep
　　'Neath a bright green covering,
Slender shades of tender blades
　　Over us are hovering.

Fragrant sheaves of floweret leaves
　　Sweetest odors fling to us,
Merry birds with music-words
　　Perch aloft and sing to us.

Butterflies, with wings of eyes,
　　Flash a kindly cheer to us,
Stalks of clover, like a lover,
　　Bend and whisper near to us.

And we bless, with thankfulness,
　　All the flowers you give to us,
And we greet, with feelings meet,
　　All the hours you live to us;

But while we, 'neath hill and lea,
　　Floral favors owe to you,
We above, with smiles of love,
　　Blooms of blessings throw to you.

Once we stood, in doubtful mood,
　　On a hill-top, listening—
Gazing where, supremely fair,
　　Heaven's domes were glistening:

Widowed wives, whose own good lives
    Their great grief had cost to them:
Mothers who till death were true,
    Maids whose loves were lost to them;

They who strove, with deeds of love,
    To keep back the dying ones,
Until *they* were drawn, one day,
    'Mongst the heavenward flying ones:

So we stood, in doubtful mood,
    On a hill-top, listening,
Gazing where, supremely fair,
    Heaven's domes were glistening;

Wondering why there came not nigh
    Some who all had dared for us,
Sad together wondering whether
    Our sweet dead yet cared for us !

At a sound we turned around:
    They had stolen near to us,
They whom we had yearned to see—
    They who were so dear to us;

So, while you these heroes true
    Praise, and with flowers cover them,
We above throw looks of love,
    And caresses, over them.

## III.

Men who fell at a loss,
    Who died 'neath failure's frown,
Who carried Strife's red cross,
    And gained not Victory's crown,
Whose wrong fight was so brave
    That it won our sad applause,

Who sleep in a hero's grave,
    Though clutched by the corpse of a cause:
Sleep sweet! with no misgiving,
    By bitter memories fed,
That we, your foes when living,
    Can be your foes when dead.
Your fault shall not e'en be spoken;
    You paid for it on the pall;
The shroud is Forgiveness' token,
    And Death makes saints of all.
Your land has in its keeping
    Our brothers, doomed to die:
Their souls went upward, sweeping
    Through storms of a southern sky;
The dead sons of our mothers
    Reach for your hands of clay;
So we, with your living brothers,
    Would clasp glad hands to-day;
That this young Queen of Nations,
    As famous as the sun,
Which has lived through tribulations
    A hundred years and one,
Shall wrap the centuries round her
    Again and yet again,
Till their gleaming braids have wound her
    In a thousand years and ten!

### [RESPONSE.]

From our dead foemen comes no chiding forth;
We lie at peace; Heaven has no South or North.
With roots of tree and flower and fern and heather,
God reaches down, and clasps our hands together.

### IV.

Men of the dark-hued race,
    Whose freedom meant—to die—
Who lie, with pain-wrought face
    Upturned to the peaceful sky,

Whose day of jubilee,
 So many years o'erdue,
Came—but only to be
 A day of death to you;
The flowers of whose love grew bright,
 E'en in Oppression's track,
The mills of whose hearts ran right,
 Though under a roof of black;
Crushed of a martyred race,
 Jet-jewelry of your clan,
You showed with what good grace
 A man may die for man.
To cringe and toil and bleed,
 Your sires and you were born;
You grew in the ground of greed,
 You throve in the frost of scorn!
But now, as your fireless ashes
 Feed Liberty's fruitful tree,
The black race proudly flashes
 The star-words "We are free!"
Men who died in sight
 Of the long-sought promise-land,
Would that these flowers were bright
 As your deeds are true and grand!

[ RESPONSE. ]

Oh! we had hearts, as brave and true
As those that lighter covering knew;
Love's flowers bloomed in us, pure and bright,
As if the vases were of white!

And we had homes, as sweet and rare
As if our household gods were fair;
But Death's was not the only dart
That came to force our joys apart!

And we had souls, that saw the sky,
And heard the angels singing nigh;

12

But oft in gloom those souls would set,
As if God had not found them yet!

Columbia brought us from afar—
She chained us to her triumph-car;
She drove us, fettered, through the street,
She lashed us, toiling at her feet!

We prayed to her, as prone we lay;
She turned her scornful face away!
She glanced at us, when sore afraid;
We rose, and hurried to her aid!

White faces sunk into the grave—
Black faces, too—and all were brave;
Their red blood thrilled Columbia's heart—
It could not tell the two apart.


## V.

Boys, whose glossy hair
    Grows gray in the age of the grave,
Who lie so humble there,
    Because you were strong and brave;
You, whose lives cold set
    Like a Winter sun ill-timed,
Whose hearts ran down ere yet
    The noon of your lives had chimed;
You, who in the sun
    Of girlhood's smiles were basking,
Who left fresh hearts all won—
    White hands to be had for asking,
You, whose bright true faces
    Are dimmed with clouds of dust,
Who hide in the gloomy places,
    And cringe in the teeth of rust;
Do you know your fathers are near,
    The wrecks of their pride to meet?

"DREAMING WHAT ROYAL LOVERS SUCH LOVERS AS YOU WOULD BE."

Do you know your mothers are here,
    To throw their hearts at your feet?
Do you know the maiden hovers
    O'er you, with bended knee,
Dreaming what royal lovers
    Such lovers as you would be?
Ruins of youthful graces,
    Strong buds crushed in Spring,
Lift up your phantom faces,
    And see the flowers we bring.


[ RESPONSE. ]

We struck our camp at break of day—we marched into the fight;
We laid the rose of pleasure down, and grasped the thorns of right.

The drum's roll was joy to us; the fife was sweetly shrill;
The waving of our country's flag—it made our pulses thrill.

They cheered us as we walked the streets; they marched us to and fro;
And they who staid spoke loud to us how brave it was to go.

Our faces set with iron deeds that yet were to be done;
Our muskets clean and bright and new, and glistening in the sun;

It was so like some tournament—some grander sort of play—
That time we bravely shouldered arms, and marched, marched away!

There came a sudden dash of tears from those who said good-bye—
We set our teeth together tight, and made them no reply.

There leaped a moisture to our eyes, but Pride was there, on guard,
And would not pass the aching tears that came so fierce and hard.

'Twould never do to droop our heads so early in the fray!
So gallantly we shouldered arms, and marched, marched away.

But when the cold and cruel night about our tents did creep,
And Memory took the midnight watch, and Pride had gone to sleep,

When hard Endurance threw aside the mask that he had worn,
And all we had a day ago seemed ever from us torn,

And when the boy within us had to perish for the man,
'Twas then the holiday was done—'twas then the fight began!

Full many arts of agony can Trouble's hand employ;
And none of them but she will use upon a home-sick boy!

The old house came back to us; and every scene was there,
The bright and cheerful morning hour—the singing and the prayer;

(Before us, every olden scene in perfect outline lay;
There never was a view so clear that seemed so far away!)

The neat and tidy noon-time—the evening banquet spread—
The smiles that flew from face to face—the pleasant words we said;

The evening ramble down the road—'twas then our fight began,
When first the boy within us had to perish for the man!

The morning broke; and ere the dark retreated from the sun,
Came shuddering through the fresh air a heavy signal-gun;

And oh! it was a grand time when, through the battle's cry,
We went, to show, if needs must be, how bravely boys could die!

It seems so like some brilliant dream—that glory-painted day,
We turned our faces toward the fight, and marched, marched away!

But when, the frantic battle done, we lay amid the slain,
Our blue coats trimmed with crimson blood—our bodies stabbed with
    pain—

When, with no friend to care for us, we stretched us out to die,
Without a shelter to our heads except the distant sky;

'Twas then the agony of war, in all its woe we knew;
We ordered up our hearts' reserves, and fought the battle through!

But soon, the hand of suffering its heavy weight upbore—
And sweet Relief came near to us, and opened Heaven's door;

The spirit brave from every clime gave welcome to their band;
Old heroes smiled into our eyes, and grasped us by the hand!

We were the honored guests of Heaven—the heroes of the day;
With laurel-wreaths upon our brows, we marched, marched away!

## VI.

Sleep well, O sad-browed city!
    Whatever may betide,
Not under a nation's pity,
    But 'mid a nation's pride.
The vines that round you clamber,
    Brightest shall be, and best;
You sleep in the honor-chamber—
    Each one a royal guest.
Columbia e'er will know you,
    From out her glittering towers,
And kisses of love will throw you,
    And send you wreaths of flowers;
And e'er in realms of glory
    Shine bright your starry claims;
Angels have heard your story,
    And God knows all your names.

# SELECTED HOME READING.

**WILL CARLETON'S POETICAL WORKS.**

Illustrated. Square 8vo, Ornamental Cloth, $2 00; Gilt Edges, $2 50; Full Seal, $4 00.

| | | |
|---|---|---|
| CITY FESTIVALS. | CITY LEGENDS. | CITY BALLADS. |
| FARM FESTIVALS. | FARM LEGENDS. | FARM BALLADS. |

**CYCLOPÆDIA OF POETRY.**

Harper's Cyclopædia of British and American Poetry. Edited by EPES SARGENT. Large 8vo, Illuminated Cloth, Colored Edges, $4 50.

**POETS OF THE NINETEENTH CENTURY.**

Poets of the Nineteenth Century. Selected and Edited by the Rev. ROBERT ARIS WILLMOTT. With English and American Additions. Superbly illustrated. Small 4to, printed on Superfine Tinted Paper, Extra Cloth, Bevelled Gilt Edges, $5 00; Half Calf, $5 50; Full Turkey Morocco, $9 00.

**THE POETS OF SCOTLAND.**

The Poets and Poetry of Scotland. From the Earliest to the Present Time. Comprising Characteristic Selections from the Works of the more Noteworthy Scottish Poets, with Biographical and Critical Notices. By JAMES GRANT WILSON. With Portraits on Steel. 2 vols., 8vo, Cloth, $10 00; Cloth, Gilt Edges, $11 00; Half Calf, $14 50; Full Morocco, $18 00.

**WALLACE'S BEN-HUR.**

Ben-Hur: A Tale of the Christ. By LEW. WALLACE. *Garfield Edition.* 2 volumes. Twenty Full-page Photogravures. Over One Thousand Illustrations as Marginal Drawings by WILLIAM MARTIN JOHNSON. Crown 8vo, Silk and Gold, Uncut Edges and Gilt Tops, $7 00. (*In a Box.*)

**TENNYSON'S SONGS, WITH MUSIC.**

Songs from the Published Writings of Alfred Tennyson. Set to Music by various Composers. Edited by W. G. CUSINS. With Portrait and Original Illustrations by Winslow Homer, C. S. Reinhart, A. Fredericks, and Jessie Curtis. Royal 4to, Cloth, Gilt Edges, $5 00.

**TENNYSON'S WORKS.**

Complete Works of Alfred, Lord Tennyson. Poet-Laureate. With an Introductory Sketch by ANNE THACKERAY RITCHIE. With Portraits and Illustrations. Pages 430. 8vo, Cloth, $2 00; Gilt Edges, $2 50.

**FOLK-LORE OF SHAKESPEARE.**

Folk-Lore of Shakespeare. By the Rev. T. F. THISELTON DYER, M.A., Oxon. 8vo, Cloth, $2 50.

**DOWDEN'S SHAKSPERE.**

Shakspere: A Critical Study of his Mind and Art. By EDWARD DOWDEN, LL.D., Vice-President of "The New Shakspere Society." 12mo, Cloth, $1 75.

**GOLDSMITH'S WORKS.**

The Works of Oliver Goldsmith. Edited by PETER CUNNINGHAM, F.S.A. From New Electrotype Plates. 4 vols., 8vo, Cloth, Paper Labels, Uncut Edges and Gilt Tops, $8 00; Sheep, $10 00; Half Calf, $17 00.

## ROLFE'S ENGLISH CLASSICS.

Edited, with Notes, by W. J. ROLFE, A.M.  Illustrated.  Small 4to, Flexible Cloth, 56 cents per volume ; Paper, 40 cents per volume.

SELECT POEMS OF GOLDSMITH.—SELECT POEMS OF THOMAS GRAY.—SELECT POEMS OF ROBERT BROWNING.—BROWNING'S DRAMAS.—MILTON'S MINOR POEMS.—MACAULAY'S LAYS OF ANCIENT ROME.—WORDSWORTH'S SELECT POEMS.

SHAKESPEARE'S THE TEMPEST.—MERCHANT OF VENICE.—KING HENRY THE EIGHTH.—JULIUS CÆSAR.—RICHARD THE SECOND.—MACBETH.—MIDSUMMER NIGHT'S DREAM.—KING HENRY THE FIFTH.—KING JOHN.—AS YOU LIKE IT.—KING HENRY IV. Part I.—KING HENRY IV. Part II.—HAMLET.—MUCH ADO ABOUT NOTHING.—ROMEO AND JULIET.—OTHELLO.—TWELFTH NIGHT.—THE WINTER'S TALE.—RICHARD THE THIRD.—KING LEAR.—ALL'S WELL THAT ENDS WELL.—CORIOLANUS.—TAMING OF THE SHREW.—CYMBELINE.—THE COMEDY OF ERRORS.—ANTONY AND CLEOPATRA.—MEASURE FOR MEASURE.—MERRY WIVES OF WINDSOR.—LOVE'S LABOUR'S LOST.—TIMON OF ATHENS.—TWO GENTLEMEN OF VERONA.—TROILUS AND CRESSIDA.—HENRY VI. Part I.—HENRY VI. Part II.—HENRY VI. Part III.—PERICLES, PRINCE OF TYRE.—THE TWO NOBLE KINSMEN.—VENUS AND ADONIS, &c.—SONNETS.—TITUS ANDRONICUS.

## SHAKESPEARE'S WORKS.

Friendly Edition of Shakespeare's Works.  Edited by W. J. ROLFE.  In 20 volumes.  Illustrated.  16mo, Cloth, $25 00 ; Half Leather, $35 00 ; Half Calf, $50 00.  (*In a Box.*)

## SHAKSPEARE'S DRAMATIC WORKS.

The Dramatic Works of Shakspeare, with the Corrections and Illustrations of Dr. JOHNSON, G. STEEVENS, and others.  Revised by ISAAC REED.  Illustrated. 6 vols., Royal 12mo, Cloth, $9 00 ; Sheep, $11 40.

## SWINTON'S ENGLISH LITERATURE.

Studies in English Literature : being Typical Selections of British and American Authorship, from Shakespeare to the Present Time ; together with Definitions, Notes, Analyses, and Glossary, as an aid to Systematic Literary Study. By Professor WILLIAM SWINTON, A.M., Author of "Harper's Language Series."  With Portraits.  Crown 8vo, Cloth, $1 20.

## BRUCE'S POEMS.

Old Homestead Poems.  By WALLACE BRUCE.  Illustrated.  Square 8vo, Cloth, $2 00.

## THE BOOK OF GOLD, AND OTHER POEMS.

The Book of Gold, and Other Poems.  By J. T. TROWBRIDGE.  Illustrated. 8vo, Ornamental Covers, Gilt Edges, $2 50.

## CHRISTMAS IN SONG, SKETCH, AND STORY.

Nearly Three Hundred Christmas Songs, Hymns, and Carols.  With Selections from BEECHER, WALLACE, AUERBACH, ABBOTT, WARREN, and DICKENS. Illustrations by RAPHAEL, MURILLO, BOUGUEREAU, HOFMANN, DEFREGGER, STORY, SHEPHERD, DARLEY, MEADE, NAST, and others.  Selected by J. P. MCCASKEY, Compiler of the "Franklin Square Song Collection."  Royal 8vo, Cloth, $2 50.

## ENGLISH MEN OF LETTERS.

12mo, Cloth, 75 cents a volume. PEOPLE'S EDITION, 36 vols in 12, 16mo, Cloth, $12 00. (*Sold only in sets.*)

JOHNSON. By Leslie Stephen.—GIBBON. By J. C. Morison.—SCOTT. By R. H. Hutton.—SHELLEY. By John Addington Symonds.—HUME. By Professor Huxley.—GOLDSMITH. By William Black.—DEFOE. By William Minto.—BURNS. By Principal Shairp.—SPENSER. By Dean Church.—THACKERAY. By Anthony Trollope.—BURKE. By John Morley.—MILTON. By Mark Pattison.—SOUTHEY. By Edward Dowden.—CHAUCER. By Adolphus William Ward.—BUNYAN. By James Anthony Froude.—COWPER. By Goldwin Smith.—POPE. By Leslie Stephen.—BYRON. By John Nichol.—LOCKE. By Thomas Fowler.—WORDSWORTH. By F. W. H. Myers.—DRYDEN. By G. Saintsbury.—HAWTHORNE. By Henry James, Jr.—LANDOR. By Sidney Colvin.—DE QUINCEY. By David Masson.—LAMB. By Alfred Ainger. —BENTLEY. By R. C. Jebb.—DICKENS. By A. W. Ward.—GRAY. By E. W. Gosse.—SWIFT. By Leslie Stephen.—STERNE. By H. D. Traill.—MACAULAY. By James Cotter Morison.—FIELDING. By Austin Dobson.—SHERIDAN. By Mrs. Oliphant.—ADDISON. By W. J. Courthope.—BACON. By R. W. Church, Dean of St. Paul's.—COLERIDGE. By H. D. Traill.—SIDNEY. By J. A. Symonds.—KEATS. By Sidney Colvin. (*Other volumes in preparation.*)

## WORKS OF WILLIAM HAMILTON GIBSON.

SHARP EYES. A Rambler's Calendar of Fifty-two Weeks Among Birds, Insects, and Flowers. Profusely Illustrated. 8vo, Cloth, $5 00.

HAPPY HUNTING-GROUNDS. A Tribute to the Woods and Fields. Illustrated by the Author. 4to, Cloth, Gilt Edges, $7 50. (*In a Box.*)

HIGHWAYS AND BYWAYS; Or, Saunterings in New England. Illustrated by the Author. 4to, Cloth, Gilt Edges, $7 50. (*In a Box.*)

PASTORAL DAYS; Or, Memories of a New England Year. Superbly Illustrated. 4to, Cloth, Gilt Edges, $7 50. (*In a Box.*)

STROLLS BY STARLIGHT AND SUNSHINE. Illustrated by the Author. Royal 8vo, Cloth, Gilt Edges, $3 50.

## ENGLISH'S POETICAL WORKS.

THE BOY'S BOOK OF BATTLE LYRICS. By THOMAS DUNN ENGLISH, M.D., LL.D. Illustrated. Square 8vo, Ornamental Cloth, $2 00.

AMERICAN BALLADS. By THOMAS DUNN ENGLISH, M.D., LL.D. 32mo, Paper, 25 cents; Cloth, 40 cents.

## PERRY'S ENGLISH LITERATURE.

English Literature in the Eighteenth Century. By THOMAS SERGEANT PERRY. 12mo, Cloth, $2 00.

## SKETCHING RAMBLES IN HOLLAND.

By GEORGE H. BOUGHTON, A.R.A. Beautifully and Profusely Illustrated with Wood-engravings from Drawings by the Author and EDWIN A. ABBEY. With Two Artists' Full-page Proofs, Japanese Paper, without Letters. Square 8vo, Cloth, Uncut Edges, and Gilt Top, $5 00.

## ILLUSTRATED BY E. A. ABBEY:

"THE QUIET LIFE." Certain Verses by Various Hands; the Motive set forth in a Prologue and Epilogue by AUSTIN DOBSON; the whole adorned with numerous drawings by EDWIN A. ABBEY and ALFRED PARSONS. 4to, Ornamental Leather, $7 50. (*In a Box.*)

OLD SONGS. Illustrated by EDWIN A. ABBEY. With Decorative Designs by ALFRED PARSONS. 4to, Ornamental Leather, $7 50. (*In a Box.*)

SHE STOOPS TO CONQUER; OR, THE MISTAKES OF A NIGHT. A Comedy. By Dr. GOLDSMITH. Illustrated by EDWIN A. ABBEY. With Ten Full-page Photogravure Reproductions, printed on separate plates, and numerous Wood-engravings. Folio, Illuminated Leather, Gilt Edges, $20 00. (*In a Box.*)

SELECTIONS FROM THE POEMS OF ROBERT HERRICK. With numerous Illustrations by EDWIN A. ABBEY. 4to, Illuminated Cloth, Gilt Edges, $7 50. (*In a Box.*)

## COLERIDGE'S ANCIENT MARINER. ILLUSTRATED BY DORÉ.

The Rime of the Ancient Mariner. By SAMUEL TAYLOR COLERIDGE. Illustrated by GUSTAVE DORÉ. Folio, Cloth, $10 00.

## POE'S RAVEN. ILLUSTRATED BY DORÉ.

The Raven. By EDGAR ALLAN POE. Illustrated by GUSTAVE DORÉ. With Comment by E. C. STEDMAN. Folio (Uniform with Doré's *Ancient Mariner*), Illuminated Cloth, Gilt Edges, and in a neat Box, $10 00.

## DORÉ'S LONDON.

London: A Pilgrimage. Illustrations by GUSTAVE DORÉ. Letter-press by BLANCHARD JERROLD. Folio, Cloth, $5 00.

## ILLUSTRATED BY ALFRED PARSONS:

A SELECTION FROM THE SONNETS OF WILLIAM WORDSWORTH. With numerous Illustrations by ALFRED PARSONS. 4to, Full Leather, Gilt Edges, $5 00. (*In a Box.*)

THE WARWICKSHIRE AVON. Notes by A. T. QUILLER-COUCH. Illustrations by ALFRED PARSONS. 8vo, Ornamental Half Leather, $2 00.

## ART AND CRITICISM.

Monographs and Studies. By THEODORE CHILD. Profusely Illustrated. Large 8vo, Cloth, $6 00.

## AMERICAN ARCHITECTURE.

Studies. By MONTGOMERY SCHUYLER. With Illustrations. pp. ix., 211. 8vo, Full Leather, Ornamental, Uncut Edges, and Gilt Top, $2 50.

## NAST'S CHRISTMAS DRAWINGS.

Thomas Nast's Christmas Drawings for the Human Race. pp. 130. 4to, Cloth, $2 00.

---

PUBLISHED BY HARPER & BROTHERS, NEW YORK.

☞ HARPER & BROTHERS *will send any of the foregoing works by mail, postage prepaid, to any part of the United States, Canada, or Mexico, on receipt of the price.*